JAMES HOGG

A Series of

Lay Sermons

on

Good Principles and Good Breeding

edited by
Gillian Hughes

with a note on the text by
Douglas S. Mack

EDINBURGH UNIVERSITY PRESS

1997

© Edinburgh University Press, 1997

Edinburgh University Press
2 George Square
Edinburgh
EH8 9LF

Typeset at the University of Stirling
Printed by The University Press, Cambridge

ISBN 0 7486 0746 3

A CIP record for this book is available
from the British Library

The Stirling / South Carolina Research Edition of

The Collected Works of James Hogg

The Aims of the Edition

James Hogg lived from 1770 till 1835. He was regarded by his contemporaries as one of the leading writers of the day, but the nature of his fame was influenced by the fact that, as a young man, he had been a self-educated shepherd. The third edition (1814) of his poem *The Queen's Wake* contains an 'Advertisement' which begins as follows.

The Publisher having been favoured with letters from gentlemen in various parts of the United Kingdom respecting the Author of the *Queen's Wake*, and most of them expressing doubts of his being a Scotch Shepherd, he takes this opportunity of assuring the public, that *The Queen's Wake* is really and truly the production of *James Hogg*, a common Shepherd, bred among the mountains of Ettrick Forest, who went to service when only seven years of age; and since that period has never received any education whatever.

The view of Hogg taken by his contemporaries is also reflected in the various early reviews of *The Private Memoirs and Confessions of a Justified Sinner*, which appeared anonymously in 1824. As Gillian Hughes has shown in the *Newsletter of the James Hogg Society* no. 1, many of these reviews identify Hogg as the author, and see the novel as presenting 'an incongruous mixture of the strongest powers with the strongest absurdities'. The Scotch Shepherd was regarded as a man of powerful and original talent, but it was felt that his lack of education caused his work to be marred by frequent failures in discretion, in expression, and in knowledge of the world. Worst of all was Hogg's lack of what was called 'delicacy', a failing which caused him to deal in his writings with subjects (such as prostitution) which were felt to be unsuitable for mention in polite literature. Hogg was regarded as a man of undoubted genius, but his genius was felt to be seriously flawed.

A posthumous collected edition of Hogg was published in the late 1830s. As was perhaps natural in the circumstances, the publishers (Blackie & Son of Glasgow) took pains to smooth away what they took to be the rough edges of Hogg's writing, and to remove his numerous 'indelicacies'. This process was taken even further in the 1860s, when the Rev. Thomas Thomson prepared a revised edition of Hogg's *Works* for publication by Blackie. These Blackie editions present a bland and lifeless version of Hogg's writings. It was in this version that Hogg was read by the Victorians. Unsurprisingly, he came to be regarded as a minor figure, of no great importance or interest.

The second half of the twentieth century has seen a substantial revival of Hogg's reputation; and he is now generally considered to be one of Scotland's major writers. This new reputation is based on a few works which have been republished in editions based on his original texts. Nevertheless, a number of Hogg's major works remain out of print. Indeed, some have been out of print for more than a century and a half, while others, still less fortunate, have never been published at all in their original, unbowdlerised condition.

Hogg is thus a major writer whose true stature was not recognised

in his own lifetime because his social origins led to his being smoth-
ered in genteel condescension; and whose true stature has not been
recognised since, because of a lack of adequate editions. The poet
Douglas Dunn wrote of Hogg in the *Glasgow Herald* in September 1988:
'I can't help but think that in almost any other country of Europe a
complete, modern edition of a comparable author would have been
available long ago'. The Stirling / South Carolina Edition of James
Hogg seeks to fill the gap identified by Douglas Dunn. When com-
pleted the edition will run to thirty-one volumes; and it will cover
Hogg's prose, his poetry, and his plays.

Acknowledgements

The research for the first volumes of the Stirling / South Carolina
Edition of James Hogg has been sustained by funding and other support generously made available by the University of Stirling and by
the University of South Carolina. In addition, funding of crucial importance was received through the Glenfiddich Living Scotland Awards;
this was particularly pleasant and appropriate, given Hogg's well-known
delight in good malt whisky. Valuable grants or donations have also
been received from the Carnegie Trust for the Universities of Scotland, from the Association for Scottish Literary Studies, and from the
James Hogg Society. The work of the Edition could not have been
carried on without the support of these bodies. In addition, my sincere
thanks to Micah Gilbert and Alys Wilman for invaluable assistance
with typesetting.

Douglas S. Mack
General Editor

Volume Editor's Acknowledgements

The present volume could not have been prepared without the help of
a number of people. Douglas Mack, besides preparing the Note on the
Text, suggested various improvements to the Introduction and Notes
and provided much-valued support. Peter Garside, with his usual generosity, read drafts of the Introduction and Notes, and made many
detailed and valuable suggestions. I also wish to thank Nigel and Priscilla
Bawcutt, Barbara Bloedé, Valentina Bold, Wilma Mack, Robin

MacLachlan, Silvia Mergenthal, Jill Rubenstein, Patrick Scott, and David Sweet. I am also grateful to the following institutions for permission to cite Hogg's manuscript materials in their care: The Beinecke Rare Book and Manuscript Library, Yale University; Biggar Museum Trust; The Historical Society of Pennsylvania; the Trustees of the National Library of Scotland; the Society of Antiquaries of Scotland and the Trustees of the National Museums of Scotland.

Gillian Hughes

Contents

Introduction xi

A Series of Lay Sermons

Sermon I. Good Principles 5

"Why will you bring down my grey hairs with sorrow to
the grave?"

Sermon II. Young Women 16

"Because the daughters of Zion are haughty, and walk with
stretched-forth necks and wanton eyes, walking and mincing as they go, and making a tinkling with their feet. * * * In
that day the Lord will take away the bravery of their tinkling ornaments about their feet, and their cauls and their
round tires like the moon, the chains, and the bracelets, and
the mufflers, the bonnets, and the ornaments of the legs,
and the headbands, and the tablets, and the ear-rings, the
rings, and the nose-jewels, the changeable suits of apparel,
and the mantles, and the wimples, and the crisping-pins, the
glasses, and the fine linen, and the hoods, and the vails."

Sermon III. Good Breeding 28

"A wholesome tongue is a tree of life; but perverseness therein
is a breach in the spirit."

Sermon IV. Soldiers 40

"From whence come wars and fighting among you? Sirs, ye
are brethren; why do ye harm one to another?"

Sermon V. To Young Men 48

"My son, if sinners entice thee, consent thou not."

Sermon VI. Reason and Instinct 58
"I pray God your whole spirit, and soul, and body, be preserved blameless."

Sermon VII. To Parents 68
"Train up a child in the way he should go."

Sermon VIII. Virtue the Only Source of Happiness . . 81
"Happy is that people whose God is the Lord."

Sermon IX. Marriage 91
"It is better to marry than to burn."

Sermon X. Reviewers 99
"O that mine enemy had written a book!"

Sermon XI. Deistical Reformers 108
"The fool hath said in his heart, there is no God."

Note on the Text (Douglas S. Mack) 121

Notes 123

Introduction

1. The Genesis of *Lay Sermons*.

Among the books advertised as 'published this day' on 19 April 1834 was *A Series of Lay Sermons on Good Principles and Good Breeding. By the Ettrick Shepherd*, a duodecimo volume costing seven shillings and brought out by James Fraser of 215 Regent Street in London.[1] James Fraser is chiefly remembered nowadays as the publisher of *Fraser's Magazine*, begun in 1830 as a more or less avowed imitation of *Blackwood's Edinburgh Magazine* in its earlier, wilder days. William Maginn, responding to an accusation of imitation, attributed this to their use of the same contributors, and added, 'There was once a time, indeed, when our *northern model*, as the blockhead calls *Blackwood*, bore a nearer resemblance to ours than he does now: we allude to the high and palmy days, the days of *Ebony's* juvenescence [...]'.[2] Hogg's own services had been requested as early as February 1830 and he was a regular and enthusiastic contributor until the end of his life, describing the magazine as 'a capital work', one which 'should succeed to a boundless extent'.[3] More than a dozen of Hogg's tales were published in *Fraser's*, as well as around twenty of his poems and songs, in the few years between its inception and the end of his life. When his quarrel with William Blackwood at the end of 1831 formally closed the pages of the Edinburgh magazine to Hogg's work *Fraser's Magazine* replaced it as the most important outlet for his periodical contributions. During his London visit of 1832 Hogg socialised with a number of *Fraser's* contributors, its effective editor William Maginn, and its publisher, and could feel himself once again, despite the distance of Altrive from London, a member of a band of literary companions centred around a magazine. Hogg's connection with *Fraser's Magazine* presumably paved the way for James Fraser's publication of a separate work by him.

Unfortunately the parallel between Blackwood and Fraser breaks down when an attempt is made to trace more directly the genesis of *Lay Sermons*: there is no Fraserian equivalent of the indispensable Blackwood archives, in which the correspondence between Hogg and his publisher charts the growth of the work and the modifications which it has undergone at the hands of each party up to the moment of publication, as there is, for example, in the case of a Blackwood book such as *The Shepherd's Calendar*.[4] Hogg certainly corresponded with James Fraser but only a handful of their letters have survived. Neither is there any surviving manuscript material to enable a partial reconstruction of the process by comparing it with the first edition of the work, as there is, for example, in the case of *Tales of the Wars of Montrose*.[5] The precise details of the genesis of *Lay Sermons* must probably, therefore, remain largely unknown. Only a few indications are accessible through careful speculation, based on the internal evidence of the work itself and on what isolated portions of the relevant correspondence have survived.

The Preface to *Lay Sermons* is dated 31 March 1834: this forms part of the book's preliminaries, normally the section of a book to be printed last, but there are numerous other internal indications that the work was written not long before its date of publication, late in Hogg's writing career. Hogg's 1832 London visit as well as the conversational powers of his friend Sir Walter Scott are both discussed in the past tense (pp.30, 33, 29), for example. He mentions the heresy of Rowism (p.109), condemned by the Church of Scotland by means of the deposition of the minister of Rowe or Rhu in 1831, and describes himself as having mixed in all classes of society for 'upwards of twenty years' (p.82). This last statement, taken in conjunction with his earlier one that he entered into genteel society in 1813 (p.48), would seem to indicate that Hogg is probably writing no earlier than 1833. Certainly by 25 January 1834 Fraser appears to have been in the process of having the book printed, for in a letter of that date enumerating his works for possible republication in America Hogg includes 'a volume of Sermons on good principles and good breeding now in the London press', which is 'still in proof'.[6] Hogg's firm description of the work as 'in proof' may imply that he had recently seen those proofs himself, which in turn suggests that the bulk of his manuscript (though not the Preface, with a date subsequent to this letter) was probably in Fraser's hands by the end of 1833. Again, almost nothing is known about the terms upon which Fraser published the work, the number of copies printed, and the remuneration Hogg was to receive as its author. In writing to Fraser on 14 September 1835 to enquire about the possibility of putting out the remaining copies as a second edition or publishing an actual second edition Hogg says 'but as you are not bound to me by any bargain except what friendship and honour dictates just do as you like'.[7] Clearly the terms for publishing a second edition had never been established, but the letter may also indicate an uncharacteristic imprecision about the conditions on which Hogg had offered Fraser the original manuscript. No surviving record has been traced

of a payment or payments made by Fraser to Hogg for *Lay Sermons,*
which does not of course indicate that none was made.

Hogg's relations with Fraser during 1833 were darkened by a serious, if short-lived, quarrel over the presentation of the Ettrick Shepherd in *Fraser's Magazine,* and this has its significance for *Lay Sermons.* It
is richly ironic that William Blackwood, who had gleefully included
Wilson's 'Noctes Ambrosianae' with their depiction of the Ettrick Shepherd as boozing buffoon in *Blackwood's Edinburgh Magazine,* had tried to
dissuade Hogg from becoming a contributor to the rival London periodical on the grounds that it contained articles showing him personal
disrespect. As Hogg told Fraser in his letter of 2 June 1830, 'Mr
Blackwood is very ill pleased about it and says that I have as good
reason to be so from Mr Cunningham's letter on the hustings however I am long ago rendered callous to all jokes'. In the article alluded
to by Blackwood the contributors to the new magazine meet to elect its
editor, and Hogg is one of the comical candidates for office.[8] In general the new magazine's attitude to Hogg was a curious mixture of
warm praise and ridicule, motivated by a desire to take up the cudgels
on his behalf against the rival *Blackwood's* and yet enjoy the comic po-
tentialities of the *Blackwood's* Shepherd. For example, a single article
could state that Hogg is 'a remarkable man, and worthy to be talked of
[...] in terms less vague than serve to create a laugh in a bantering
periodical' and also draw an imaginary picture of the Shepherd danc-
ing, with the comment 'if he would not wallop like a satyr, we are deaf
and know nothing: and then with what grace might he *allemand* in a
quadrille, with his frieze coat and shepherd's brogues'.[9] Hogg's general desire to bring the persona of the Ettrick Shepherd back under his
own control is demonstrated in his writing of a number of Noctes-type
dialogues from the late 1820s onwards: his two 'Noctes Bengerianae'
appeared in the *Edinburgh Literary Journal,* for example, while 'Dr David
Dale's Account of a Grand Aerial Voyage' in the same periodical had
originally been intended to appear in *Blackwood's* itself as a 'Noctes'
written by the Shepherd.[10] In the summer of 1833 he wrote two papers
as a new series of the 'Noctes Ambrosianae' for *Fraser's Magazine,* presumably hoping to take advantage of the London periodical's rivalry
with *Blackwood's* and to regain control of the Shepherd within that context. Fraser's letter of 26 June 1833 explains why they were not acceptable for inclusion in his magazine, nicknamed Regina:

> Your mind seems bent upon continuing the Noctes in Regina
> and I am very sorry to thwart you in the matter but I have not
> come to my present conclusion until much consideration nor until
> the advice of my best advisers (especially the two to whom you

referred me—Doctor Maginn & William Fraser—) has been taken
upon the subject.

    I found that few would wade thro' your MSS so I had the first
set up in type trusting that a favourable opinion would be given
in behalf of the plan & that it could be used—all liked the composition—for my own part I think it inimitable & equal to any of
Blackwoods—but all were against Regina stooping to an imitation—Being unwilling to lose it entirely the Doctor kindly offered
to concoct from it a short paper which I have enclosed & which
will appear in the July number [...] I trust you will take the Doctor's hint & give us a series of Epistolae Hoggi the idea is admira-
ble & affords you as fine a field as any four of conversations ever
could do[11]

Maginn's writing and Fraser's publishing of 'The Shepherd's Noctes,
and the reason why they do not appear in Fraser's Magazine', however, proved a serious annoyance to Hogg.[12] Without his own consent
he appeared as a dishonest and unscrupulous appropriator of the work
of a number of young song-writers who were his particular protégés,
as he explained to one of them, the composer Peter M'Leod:

I wrote a Noctes Ambrosianae for Frazer the dialogue of which
was between you Henry Riddell Gilfillan and me and each are
made to sing your own songs and explanations are given regarding both authors and composers. But the blockheads not daring
to follow up Blackwood left out the dialogue altogether and published only the songs so that the whole of them have been received as mine. I wanted to bring them all forward to notice but
owing to the absurdity of an editor I have failed and I assure you
instead of being an error of heart it was exactly the reverse. I am
exceedingly vexed about it [...].[13]

Once again Hogg's Ettrick Shepherd persona was disgracing James
Hogg, misrepresenting him when seized and controlled by another
person. He was evidently angry enough to break with James Fraser
and the magazine for several months, for Fraser, in a letter of 18 November 1833, expresses his relief at the renewal of Hogg's correspondence, saying 'I knew your goodness of heart would sooner or later
forgive a little indiscretion I might have been guilty of—and believe me
it gave me great pleasure to receive once more a letter in your own
hand & in the same kind strain as ever'.[14] The most obvious relevance
of this breach in friendly relations between July and November 1833
is in dating the *Lay Sermons*, which from internal evidence seem not to
have been written before 1833: it is now clear that Hogg would not

have sent his manuscript to Fraser for publication between July and November of that year. But the breach may have a wider significance in the possible genesis of a work with the full title of *A Series of Lay Sermons on Good Principles and Good Breeding. By the Ettrick Shepherd*. If Hogg sent his manuscript to James Fraser after November then the work may be partly a direct response to Maginn's tampering with his proposed 'Noctes'. Even if he sent his manuscript to Fraser before July, however, it was sent within the context of a long-standing attempt by *Fraser's Magazine* to appropriate and control Hogg's Ettrick Shepherd persona, and Hogg's resentment of one of the unfortunate consequences of such appropriation was clearly demonstrated within that same year.

2. The Literary Context.

The title of Hogg's work is probably somewhat off-putting to a modern reader, who is not in the habit of reading overtly religious literature and is perhaps inclined to consider such works stupefyingly dull, but to Hogg's pre-Victorian contemporaries it must have seemed rather a promising title. There was clearly a lucrative demand for religious and improving works of all kinds: young ladies, as Hogg points out in *Lay Sermons* (p.26), might be expected to read sermons at home besides attending church on Sundays, while Annuals such as the *Amulet* contained a remunerative mixture of evangelical feeling and light reading. In writing tales and poems such as 'The Cameronian Preacher's Tale', 'A Tale of Pentland', or 'A Lay of the Martyrs' Hogg was catering for his reader's desire for entertaining reading with a flavour of religious and moral improvement.[15] When he visited London at the start of 1832 he published a booklet of prayers and hymns for children entitled *A Father's New Year's Gift*, and at the time of his death was in the process of compiling a work entitled *The Young Lady's Sabbath Companion*.[16] People's attention would be aroused, therefore, when they learned that the Ettrick Shepherd was about to publish a volume of sermons. Robert Gilfillan, for example, added a quizzing postscript to his letter to Hogg of 24 March 1834 saying 'What of your *Sermons*? My *reverend* friend, shall it according to Burns "Perhaps turn out a Song perhaps turn out a Sermon!"—*Respond* R.G.'[17] There was evidently an intriguing tension for Hogg's contemporaries in the full title of the work, between the sober promise of instructive sermons and the entertainment value of the Ettrick Shepherd.

What was Hogg really offering in *A Series of Lay Sermons on Good Principles and Good Breeding. By the Ettrick Shepherd?* The eleven sermons of Hogg's collection are clearly not reprints of spoken discourse given from a pulpit, for they are the sermons of a layman and not of a cleric, but each is introduced like a sermon by a text or texts from the Bible, which is reiterated at intervals throughout the essay, and sometimes restated at its conclusion. In other words Hogg is translating into written form an essentially oral experience, just as he did, for example, in presenting the culture and orally-transmitted tales of his own Border background to the literate audience of such written works as *The Shepherd's Calendar*.

Samuel Taylor Coleridge, who had been originally intended for a Unitarian minister, had a similar idea. When he settled at Highgate in 1816 he projected a series of three lay sermons on the problems of Britain in the post-Napoleonic era. The first, entitled *The Statesman's Manual, or The Bible the Best Guide to Political Skill and Foresight. A Lay Sermon Addressed to the Higher Classes of Society* was published in December 1816, and was followed in March of the next year by *A Lay Sermon Addressed to the Higher and Middle Classes on the Existing Distresses and Discontents*. The third sermon (never actually written) was supposed to be addressed 'to the Lower and Labouring Classes of Society'.[18] It is impossible to say whether or not Hogg knew of Coleridge's two published *Lay Sermons*. He certainly knew about Coleridge himself, having parodied his work in the 'Isabelle' of *The Poetic Mirror* (1816). Coleridge was also an important influence on the early *Fraser's Magazine*, and is featured among its supporters in the print of 'The Fraserians', in which context Hogg irreverently referred to him as 'old greasy deranged Coleridge'.[19] It is possible that Hogg may have been aware of Coleridge's *Lay Sermons* through his one-time literary associate John Gibson Lockhart, for in 1819 Coleridge inscribed and annotated a copy of the 1817 sermon for Lockhart as the author of *Peter's Letters to his Kinsfolk*, a work which in turn contains a portrayal of the Ettrick Shepherd.[20] However, even though it is not possible to show that Coleridge's *Lay Sermons* were a direct influence on Hogg's own *Lay Sermons*, a brief examination of Coleridge's work may prove helpful in illuminating certain characteristics of the genre.

Firstly, the giver of a sermon is commonly allowed to be as plain-spoken as he chooses without giving offence to his audience: his object is to instruct them in their religious and moral duties and so he is absolved from the common rules of politeness that govern other forms of social discourse. Coleridge declared that in giving his work the name of a sermon he 'sought to prepare the inquirers after it for the absence of all the usual softenings suggested by worldly prudence, of all compromise between truth and courtesy'.[21] This is an important assumption for several of Hogg's sermons, particularly 'Sermon II. Young Women', where Hogg is thus free to attack the superficial education of

the typical middle-class girl of his day despite the chivalrous indulgence such girls expected and were accustomed to receive and his own
much-advertised affection for the ladies. 'If a blunt man may use a
plain expression to you' he declares, 'it is owing to the attentions of
this important period that we find so many beautiful and agreeable
women more ignorant than they should be', and adds 'the only difference between the girl and the woman is a little difference in stature,
and perhaps comeliness of form' (p.17). Again, in giving his views on
the training and education of children in 'Sermon VII. To Parents'
Hogg indicates that he is obliged to speak out and give his real views:
'as a pupil of nature, I must speak out my sentiments. I have a great
aversion to college education; indeed, I hold it in utter contempt—'
(p.76). The sermoniser is indeed in an equivalent position to the father
whom Hogg describes as being liberated from certain forms of criticism because of his function as an educator:

> Every one attaches a considerable degree of respect to the vener-
> able name of father; and his important charge makes us bear his
> superior strictness and caution without envy; and we never call
> him precise even when he descends to the minutiæ of fair and
> honourable conduct. He has, then, [...] the consent of mankind to
> be as virtuous as he pleases. (p.69)

Another characteristic of Coleridge's *Lay Sermons* is their constant stream
of Biblical reference, allusion, and quotation, and what he describes as
'a sober and meditative accomodation to your own times and country
of those important truths declared in the inspired writings'.[22] The typical audience for a sermon, obviously, is largely composed of Christians. A sermon is expected to be an address by a Christian who as-
sumes his audience's familiarity with the Bible and receptivity to a
Christian world-view. Coleridge can even seem oddly fundamentalist
at times in drawing parallels between events in biblical and present
times, for example in declaring that 'the Prophet Isaiah revealed the
true philosophy of the French revolution'.[23] Hogg too deploys a full
battery of biblical allusion and quotation, and derives warnings and
good examples for contemporary society from biblical events. In 'Sermon IV. Soldiers', for example, he deplores the use of full-scale war in
settling national disputes and argues that it 'would be much more conformable to what nature dictates, for kings or their ministers to fight it
out in person, or each by a champion, like the Israelites and Philistines'
(p.42). The shared assumptions of the sermon-giver and his audience
are most clearly shown, however, in the final sermon which is rather
about deistical reformers than addressed to them. Hogg and his audi-

ence are consistently grouped together as 'we' or 'us' while the deists
are 'them', an external threat which Hogg fortifies his audience to resist by providing them with appropriate strategies and arguments, as
in the following example:

> Let us make them bring, therefore, the little which they can prom-
> ise into competition with the immense sums we are to lose; and if
> they can afford us no equivalent, why should we listen to them?
> (p.115)

The lay sermon, clearly, is a direct address to an audience character-
ised by an appeal to shared values and a liberation from the ordinary
rules of politeness in the interests of truth and morality. Also, as a
preacher's discourse to his audience, it is obviously a very direct and
personal form of writing, perhaps because of its oral origins. Coleridge
was somewhat apprehensive that his work might be thought to resem-
ble 'the overflow of an earnest mind rather than an orderly premedi-
tated composition',[24] but this is likely to have been one of the form's
attractions for James Hogg, who was generally inclined to include the
character of the Ettrick Shepherd in his writings. Coleridge may have
been the Sage of Highgate, but Hogg was the Sage of Ettrick. *Lay
Sermons* contains a good deal of biographical information, and may be
seen on one level as a supplement to Hogg's *Memoir of the Author's Life*
and the two versions of his anecdotes of Scott, but like those works it
is also an exercise in image-making.

It should be remembered that in moving away from oral discourse
into the written form of a book the lay sermon was inevitably influenced by another tradition of improving reading, that of the essay periodical. For example, a substantial part of the introduction to
Coleridge's second *Lay Sermon* consists of an allegorical vision: he adopts
the metaphor of life as a voyage or journey, which made its way from
the Bible (and no doubt various homilies and sermons) through
Bunyan's *The Pilgrim's Progress* into the essay periodical tradition. No.
102 of Johnson's *The Rambler*, for example, entitled 'The voyage of life'
is a dream allegory on launching into the ocean of life and employs
images of boats and shipwrecks. Coleridge's debt to the tradition in
the following passage is clear:

> For these are the keystone of that arch on which alone we can
> cross the torrent of life and death with safety on the passage; with
> peace in the retrospect; and with hope shining upon us from
> through the cloud, toward which we are travelling.[25]

And Hogg in his *Lay Sermons* participates in the same tradition and employs similar imagery:

> Take a prospect of human life through the vista of reason, and you must perceive that it is a voyage to an undiscovered country. Our provisions wear out, and the vessel turns crazy as we advance. It is a voyage which we have begun, and which we should try to bring to as happy and prosperous a termination as possible. What, then, can we do better than to lay in a good store of provisions, to have honest and true messmates, and with all our skill to steer clear of the quicksands which would swallow us up, and the rocks on which we may be dashed to pieces. With these precautions, Providence for our pilot, and religion for our sheet-anchor, we shall enter the harbour with hope, and look back on the dangers that we have escaped with pleasure and exultation. (p.7)

Hogg also employs this metaphor in 'Sermon V. To Young Men', in counselling them on their choice of friends (p.49). Hogg was clearly aware of Johnson as a literary precursor in the earlier part of his writing career, both in his various written Highland tours and of course in his own essay-periodical, *The Spy*, of 1810-11. Indeed at least one paper in *The Spy* teases the reader by incorporating passages taken directly from *The Rambler*.[26] This particular kind of playfulness is not a feature of Hogg's *Lay Sermons*, but many of the topics Hogg chooses to discuss in them had also been of interest to Johnson, whose famous periodical includes discussions of marriage, old age, friendship, and the cruelty of parental tyranny, a comparison of the soul of man with the instinct of animals, and a concern with the problems of authorship, the nature of genius, and the influence of critics and criticism.[27] In other words, the themes of Hogg's *Lay Sermons* are the easily recognisable themes of the essay-periodical tradition, especially as it had been developed by Johnson. Hogg would undoubtedly have expected his reader of 1834 to recognise the literary context of *Lay Sermons* as including both the Christian sermon and the essay periodical tradition.

3. Portrait of the Sage of Ettrick.

Although *Lay Sermons* is a highly personal work and an obvious quarry for the biographer, Hogg himself could not have intended it to be read as a naive transcript of his life-experience, for his Preface gives a determined signal to the alert reader that this work shares the qualities and strategies of much of his fiction. It is a surprisingly playful introduc-

tion to a volume of sermons, and mockingly exemplifies some of the
more dubious characteristics of the Shepherd persona, as developed in
Blackwood's and imitated in *Fraser's*. The Shepherd's opening sentence
displays his vanity in announcing the likelihood that 'after the publication of this volume I shall be called to fill a chair of moral philosophy in some one of the cities of the United States, or Oxford at least'
(p.3). He explains that its 'most valuable maxims and observations'
are in fact the work of someone else, 'taken from a MS. translation of
the works of an old French monk of the last century' (p.3), and in
saying so openly casts doubt upon his own veracity and literary honesty:

> I have now given so many tales of *perfect truth* to the public,
> many of them with not one word of truth in them, that I know I
> shall not be believed in this, and that people will say, 'Oho! this is
> a mere subterfuge of the Shepherd's to get off, in case of any
> unsound tenets or instances of bad taste.' It is, nevertheless, liter-
> ally true; and I shall tell you how it came to my hand, which was
> not in a very fair way. (p.3)

It appears that Hogg is working extraordinarily hard here to discredit
himself as a sermon-giver: he is a creator of fictions, who has often
claimed that his tales are true although they are not, and the basis of
his sermons is someone else's work which he has obtained 'not in a
very fair way'. He also implies that the Shepherd's sermons may well
be unorthodox from a religious view and in bad taste from a social
one, and all this within the context of a genre which implies religious
and moral probity and earnest plain-dealing on behalf of the speaker.
His explanation of how he came into the possession of the manuscript
upon which his work is based follows:

> In 1801 I sent a MS. volume of songs, ballads, &c. to a book-
> seller in Edinburgh (many years since deceased) to publish for
> me, which he had promised to do. A long time after, he returned
> a parcel, with a letter, saying the work would not do, and for my
> own credit he had abstained from publishing it. It was this trans-
> lation which he returned me, and being greatly chagrined I kept
> it. (p.3)

As Silvia Mergenthal points out,[28] the anecdote establishes that the
speaker of *Lay Sermons* shares the life-experience of James Hogg, who
published his first collection of poetry, *Scottish Pastorals* in 1801. The
reader is suspended between biographical fact and the obviously fictive
device of the discovered manuscript, a characteristic of the Gothic novel

and an allusion which is reinforced by the reference to the old monk. Hogg is perhaps also alluding to the discovered manuscripts of his own fictions: Robert Wringhim's confessions in *The Private Memoirs and Confessions of a Justified Sinner*, Isaac the curate's original version of *The Three Perils of Man*, or Archibald Sydeserf's autobiography in 'Some Remarkable Passages in the Life of An Edinburgh Baillie. Written by himself' from *Tales of the Wars of Montrose*. As Mergenthal indicates, Hogg's claim that his story is 'literally true' is itself a piece of word-play between what is true in a historical or biographical sense and what is true in literature or 'in letters'.[29] Hogg's Preface claims on the surface to set the record straight and to explain to the reader exactly what he has been given in the volume that follows, but it really does nothing of the kind—the reader's expectations of an introduction to a collection of sermons are flouted, and he is suspended between fiction and biography. Hogg is clearly playing games: he presents the Noctean Shepherd to the reader—vain, untruthful, dishonest, and naive—as the supposed author of the sermons which are to follow, and hints that perhaps another author is to be detected.

It is no coincidence that the first sermon (immediately following Hogg's Preface), although given the heading 'Good Principles', is re-ally about old age and in particular his own experience of it. Hogg works hard to establish, by an accumulation of details, a more serious portrait of the sermon-giver. This Shepherd is calmly reflective and slightly melancholic, in Johnsonian style, about his own mortality:

> I freely tell you that I have struggled against every suggestion concerning my age; yet I cannot help occasionally stating to my-self the probable termination of my life, calculating how many years are likely to elapse before I reach it, and then grasping in my mind the space of as many years which are past. The imagi-nary period, indeed, is still to come, but I have a standard by which I can measure it; and if I were wise, I might know what it will be. (pp.5-6)

He is the adviser of his neighbours in conjunction with 'their worthy pastor' (p.7), and when in the company of young men finds 'many occasions of infusing the experience of age under the guise of equality' (p.11). Although he may appear a melancholy subject, he implies, as 'a man advanced in years with a family about him, whom he can never expect to see settled in the world' (p.7) he is nevertheless an advocate for late marriages as the 'children of an old man give youth and life to his mind' (p.7). In this self-portrait the Shepherd is prima-rily the sober family man of Altrive, partly retired from his career as a poet (p.8) but a firm advocate for exercise of both body and mind to ensure a vigorous and happy old age (p.10). Having drawn this careful outline Hogg is then able to reintroduce some of the personal characteristics he shared with the magazine Shepherd as harmless and essentially unimportant foibles. The naive vanity of the Shepherd, for example, allows him to describe himself favourably with an appearance of innocence in advising other old men upon the basis of his own experience. He tells them to mix with young people

> especially if you have any thing in your countenance or manners which invites all the young people of the families in which you visit to flock about you, hang about you, and use every familiarity with you. This is delightful, and an infallibly good sign of an old man; for it is a curious fact, that children are the best judges of character at first sight in the world. (p.11)

Vanity is united with a disarming self-mockery again in the assertion that 'I have no objections to the conceit that we are extremely vigorous for our years', and it is immediately placed within a context of serious advice and reflection, 'but let us, at all events, be convinced that old age and death are fast approaching, and let us be prepared for either' (p.9). This Shepherd relishes a joke, in alluding to himself as preacher as 'this man of the mountains' (p.14); besides the Bible he quotes a proverb or a tag from Shakespeare; and generally displays himself as an attractive and plausible (if homely) moral and religious adviser, whom we may reasonably call the Sage of Ettrick.

Having established this more plausible Shepherd persona in his first sermon Hogg carefully maintains it in the ones which follow, combining the seriousness of the moral essayist with the lighter humour of the Shepherd. He adds biographical details, jokes, and a gentle teasing of the reader's expectations to the blunt advice and careful observations of this aged, kindly personality. In 'Sermon II. Young Women', for example, the Shepherd is described as almost a hermit. The young ladies, he allows, will smile at his presumption in advising them and 'say one to another that age has not cured the shepherd of his inherent vanity', but his 'years and separation from the world' give him this right and enable him to look dispassionately on their beauty (p.16). As the Shepherd Hogg pushes the moral essay towards a more colloquial and oral discourse, the friendly fireside advice given by a patriarch to a young female friend in a setting such as the one described by Burns in 'The Cottar's Saturday Night'. (Hogg's own early poem 'The Admonition' from *The Spy* employs a similar strategy.[30]) In the following rebuke, for example, Hogg compares his ignorant young middle-class female reader to a tradesman who has not served the proper apprenticeship:

> A few young women of prudence and foresight will occasionally attend to those concerns fitting them for the duties of a wife and mother, but, alas, how few! Now, consider with yourselves how a man could build a house, make a coat or a pair of shoes, without ever having tried it before. What a bungling business he would make of either! you will say. A hundred for one of you in the higher ranks of life place yourselves in the same situation the first fair opportunity that offers. (pp.17-18)

The amusing analogy, the casual interjection of 'alas, how few!', and the enumeration of the odds against the sensible girls, all approximate this passage to oral rhetoric, and Hogg even supposes the reply a young lady might make to his supposition in an actual conversation. In other passages of this sermon Hogg addresses his audience familiarly and paternally as 'my dear girls' (p.20) and 'my young countrywomen' (p.20), admits to his liking to seeing one of his own books 'in a young lady's hand whom I like' (p.21), and gives his opinions 'on the credit of a poet' (p.22).

In 'Sermon III. Good Breeding', Hogg successfully achieves the object aimed at in his various attempts to write a 'Noctes Ambrosianae' of his own. He establishes the Shepherd as the familiar associate of literary celebrities and recounts his opinions of them and of the society in which he has participated both in Edinburgh (pp.29, 33) and during his London visit of 1832 (pp.31-32, 33, 34-35). Here the Shepherd is more the critic of his company than the licensed buffoon. He gently makes fun, for example, of the trivial commonplaces of polite conversation as follows:

> I once heard a reverend professor assert, that he had of late made a very important discovery. What was it, think you? That beet radish made a pickle greatly superior to the radishes or cabbage of Savoy! (p.35)

More seriously, Scott's deference for the feelings of others and encouragement of modest merit in conversation is contrasted favourably with the brilliant self-display and moodiness of John Wilson (p.29). This combination of personal anecdote and social criticism is continued at intervals throughout the sermons which follow, so that a Nithsdale schoolboys' squabble is compared favourably to European wars (pp.41-42), and the Shepherd's naive open-hearted sincerity is

contrasted with the affectation and falsehood common in polite society. When Hogg first entered into genteel society he 'thought it the
easiest matter possible to gain the affections of every person, of whatever age, and to live in habits of intimacy and friendship with them',
but the same people who flattered him at evening parties 'would the
next day, when I addressed them in the kindest and most affectionate
way I was able, stare me in the face, and shrink from the gloveless
hand of the poor poet, without uttering a word!' (p.48). Hogg portrays
the Shepherd as vain and naive, but also insists that he is less culpable
than those who despise him.

　　In 'Sermon VI. Reason and Instinct', Hogg's Shepherd clearly recalls the narrator of his shorter magazine fiction. His opening analysis
of the nature of the soul recalls the philosophical introductions to tales
such as 'George Dobson's Expedition to Hell' in *Blackwood's Edinburgh
Magazine* or 'On the Separate Existence of the Soul' from *Fraser's*.[31] The
Shepherd portrayed by others within such magazines must often have
appeared an unlikely author of the tales they contained signed by the
Ettrick Shepherd, but here the apparent contradiction is eliminated.
Hogg gently teases the reader whom he mentioned in his Preface as
being on the look-out for 'unsound tenets' by being conventionally
orthodox himself, and by refusing even to report the controversial religious views of other people: Dr. Dunlop, he remarks, holds a plausible theory as to the seat of the soul within the body, 'but as it may not
be deemed orthodox, I do not choose to set it down here' (p.58). Hogg
then passes from theory to giving the same kind of anecdotes of his
close personal observation and experience of animals as he does in his
essays on 'Dogs' or 'Sheep' in *The Shepherd's Calendar*.[32] These entertaining stories relieve the reflective mood of the sermon without con-
tradicting its more theoretical portions: such vignettes as the lamb's
fright when reintroduced to its formerly 'rough, well-clad, comfortable mamma' after her fleece has been shorn (p.63) are delightful pieces
of Hogg's best comic writing and should be better known.

　　Thus licensed as a homely philosopher the Shepherd goes on to
give his views on education in 'Sermon VII. To Parents', 'as a father,
as one who has felt the want of it himself, and seen the effect of it in
others' (p.68). He contrasts personal observation and common sense
against the written systems of education embodied in books on the
subject, with the reflection that a man 'may improve a hint, but he will
never do any thing more than admire a system' (p.68). Again Hogg's
theories are illustrated with biographical material and amusing anecdotes of out-of-the-way characters, as in the previous sermon, and he
then engages in the contemporary debate on higher education in Scot-

land stimulated by the Royal Commission to look into the state of the Scottish universities.

Each of the remaining four sermons is of interest: there are passages which may be usefully compared with others among Hogg's better-known writings, or which make explicit views only alluded to in passing elsewhere, or which add to biographical information about Hogg or his development of the Shepherd persona. However, 'Sermon X. Reviewers' is of particular importance as it contains Hogg's ideas on the subject of creative writing itself. These ideas should, however, be looked at cautiously and within the context of Hogg's attempt in *Lay Sermons* to establish his own version of the Shepherd persona. It appears unlikely that this sermon, any more than the others, can be treated as a window into James Hogg's breast. Silvia Mergenthal suggests that in this sermon Hogg employs a narrative strategy which addresses young readers and authors on behalf of the poet against the unnecessarily regulative critic (exemplified by Francis Jeffrey), and describes Hogg's achievement as a competent though not original summary of the aesthetics of Scottish common-sense philosophy.[33] Hogg's views on the originality of genius clearly belong to a long-standing tradition which he inherited from Burns. Perhaps his debt both of idea and language to this tradition may be most concisely demonstrated by comparing his 'Sermon X. Reviewers' to a particular example of such writing, Edward Young's *Conjectures on Original Composition. In a Letter to the Author of Sir Charles Grandison* (1759). Young explains that '*Imitations* are of two kinds; one of Nature, one of Authors: The first we call *Originals*, and confine the term *Imitation* to the second'.[34] Arguing that illustrious examples intimidate the modern writer he advises him to make use of their example only in a particular fashion:

> He that imitates the divine *Iliad*, does not imitate *Homer*; but he who takes the same method, which *Homer* took, for arriving at a capacity of accomplishing a work so great. Tread in his steps to the sole Fountain of Immortality; drink where he drank, at the true *Helicon*, that is, at the breast of Nature: Imitate; but imitate not the *Composition*, but the *Man*. (Young, pp.21-22)

Hogg's advice to the young man of imagination is remarkably similar:

> [...] step back to an early age; and if the original stamina of genius is yours, the fame you covet is secure. Take the simplicity of Moses, the splendour of Job, David, and Isaiah. Take Homer, and, if you like, Hesiod, Pindar, and Ossian; and by all means William Shakespeare. In short, borrow the fire and vigour of an early period of society, when a nation is verging from barbarism into civilisa-

tion; and then you will imbibe the force of genius from its original source. Nourish the inspiration, and despise the cold rules of
criticism. (p.103)

Pindar (Young, p.30) and Shakespeare (Young, pp.81-82) are notable
examples of true and natural genius for both poets, in declaring that
the 'fire and rapidity of true genius will always overstep the cold restraints of art' (p.100) or in urging writers to 'cherish every spark of
intellectual light and heat' (Young, p.53). Rules, declares Young (p.28),
are an impediment to the strong, while Hogg asks rhetorically 'why
should the productions of genius be tied down by the chains and fetters of criticism?' (p.100). Such doctrines act of course as a defensive
mechanism for the writer who lacks formal education, making him
equal or even superior to the writer or critic who has it: Young's essay
was addressed to Samuel Richardson, the son of a joiner with little
education who became a printer as well as the founding father of the
British novel. As the Shepherd Hogg could utilise such theories to
assert his own literary equality (or even superiority) and to free himself from the pressures of his middle-class literary mentors and critics.
The best reviewer of the work of an original genius, Hogg asserts, is
the genius himself, for 'the same man whose thoughts were like lightning while composing his works, may be cool in revising them. It is
not necessary to have one head to invent and another to censure and
correct; for, certainly, the imagination which sketches the outlines is
best qualified to finish the picture' (p.101). This somewhat solipsistic
portrait of the creative writer is qualified, however, in the sermon on
reviewers by Hogg's attempt to forge a bond with the reader, cutting
out the literary middle-man, the reviewer or professional critic. Hogg
warns the reader against the party-political bias of the reviewer and
against his 'dogmatic rules' for assessing literary merit, arguing that
'taking all the reviewers within the last half century [...] how very few
of them were capable of writing a popular original work' (pp.102-03).
A young man is advised to read none of the critics 'but think and
judge for yourself' (p.103) and 'call no man your master in taste and
judgment' (p.105). The reader is to form an intimacy with the author
that is compared to a conversation:

> Sit down to your book as you would to conversation; and never
> harbour an intention of triumph over the defects of your author;
> but divest yourself of all envy, and read to be pleased, and it is
> more than probable you will be so. (p.104)

The Shepherd of the *Lay Sermons* with his direct address and colloquial
expressions invites this personal intimacy, to which the reader is now

invited to respond appropriately. Robert Kiely perceptively comments that 'Hogg's claims for art and the artist's inspiration are, in some ways, analogous to his claims for the Christian's reliance on revelation'.[35] There is a related parallel between the intrusive deist, whose notions of natural religion seek to disrupt the community of Christians, and the intrusive literary man whose notions of artistic merit seek to disrupt the intimacy of the writer and his reader. In his *Lay Sermons* Hogg uses the powerful charm of the Shepherd as Sage of Ettrick to captivate his audience and to repel the invaders of that intimacy.

4. The Reception of *Lay Sermons*.

The contemporary reviews of *Lay Sermons* are among the most positive of Hogg's writing career. Even the *British Critic*, which disapproved of lay sermons as a genre, stated that had the work been entitled Essays or Observations 'we might have praised many passages in them for the strong sense and keen acuteness which they display'.[36] There was a general feeling that this was a better volume of lay sermons than could reasonably have been expected from the Ettrick Shepherd. As the *Monthly Magazine* expressed it:

> Those who looked forward to the publication of these 'Sermons' with the hope of enjoying 'much damnable laughter' at the Shepherd's expense—and they form a not inconsiderable portion of your reading public—will find themselves, doubtless, much disappointed. Those, on the contrary, who, jealous of the fame of this worthy and excellent man, waited with pain for what they deemed would deeply injure his name, will find themselves agreeably deceived.[37]

The *Athenaeum* concurred that 'Mr. Hogg was more in earnest than we anticipated', praising his 'unaffected and plain good sense', though preferring to this 'the occasional outbreaks' of personal anecdote and gossip.[38] The review in *Johnstone's Edinburgh Magazine* by his friend and fellow-novelist Mrs Christian Isobel Johnstone must have been especially welcome to Hogg in stating that the 'book is redolent of the originality and mother-wit of Ettrick'. She singles out for praise the sermon on good breeding, 'by which the manners of the dancing-master, and the standards of the boarding-school are not to be understood, but those habits of forbearance, gentleness, courtesy, and deference which, taken together, constitute the substance of [...] politeness', and concludes by summarising the work as 'a book written by a man of undeniable genius, and of good, shrewd, sound sense to boot, in all the simplicity of wisdom, and the wisdom of simplicity'.[39] The *Literary*

Gazette thought the work 'worthy of universal popularity', adding that Hogg 'assuredly deserves all that a liberal and grateful public can do for one whose natural genius has lifted him into high and just distinction, and who has contributed so largely to the fund of general enjoyment and gratification', but chose to interpret the work as written rather by the Noctean Shepherd of Hogg's Preface than by the Sage of Ettrick of the sermons themselves. The reviewer began by taking up Hogg's own joke in the Preface that the publication of the volume would result in his preferment, declaring that 'we should not wonder to see him elevated to the episcopal bench, or made a D.D. or a Dean at least', and continued by teasing him on the 'unmatched impudence' of stating in his sermon on reviewers that no modern criticism is to be depended on, with the exclamation 'unjust and libellous Hogg!!'. This reviewer subsequently affected disappointment that the sermon on good breeding is not concerned with the selective breeding of sheep and referred to its author as 'the holy Chesterfield of Altrive' in writing of the manners of ladies and gentlemen instead.[40] Despite this mockery, however, the review made a number of lengthy quotations from the work, thus allowing it to speak for itself, and it was strongly recommended to the paper's readers.

Oddly enough the most unfavourable review of Hogg's *Lay Sermons* by far appeared in *Fraser's Magazine*, book and periodical of course both being published by James Fraser. If Hogg tried to replace the Noctean Shepherd by his own Sage of Ettrick figure in these sermons, then this magazine was plainly determined to bring that Shepherd back again. The review is cleverly managed to appear on a careless or superficial reading a kindly notice of a grossly personal and vulgar book.[41] It opens with a comical portrait of the youthful Hogg on the stool of repentance for fornication and contrasts this with the Shepherd in his old age as kirk elder, coming home after church to make himself 'half-muzzy' from toddy and a good dinner and to preach morality to his young family. The reviewer's extensive quotations from the *Lay Sermons* are gross alterations and misrepresentations of passages from that work. For example, the review ends with ten maxims supposedly taken from Hogg's sermon on the text 'It is better to marry than burn'; they all illustrate his supposed lapses from delicacy in discussing sexual concerns, and are given references to pages subsequent to page 352. Hogg's book, however, ends at page 330, and his earlier sermon on the text decorously treats the marriage state as a companionable one and discusses a proper conduct to be observed in it by the husband. Besides this unfair invention, the reviewer also alters Hogg's existing text to make personal and scandalous allusions to Lord Grey, to em-

phasise the naive and limited experience of the Shepherd, and to rein-
force its picture of a jolly convivial man trying to express himself in
moral terms essentially foreign to his nature.[42] This *Fraser's* review is
as shabby in its treatment of Hogg as Shepherd as anything in
Blackwood's, an astonishing and appalling performance as well as being
the longest contemporary critical notice of Hogg's book.

The reception of the *Lay Sermons* in Hogg's native district appears
to have been a mixed one. Hogg's daughter, Mrs Garden, related years
afterwards that Hogg presented a copy to an old woman in the parish
of Yarrow on condition that she read one of the sermons every Sunday, but her subsequent verdict was that they were 'no for Sabbath-
day's reading'. She qualifies the old woman's criticism, however, by
giving the clerical verdict of Dr. James Russell, that the 'volume breathes
a deep feeling of reverence for the doctrines of revelation, and has
many shrewd observations on human life, while it is full of good practical advice for the guidance of old and young'.[43] Hogg seems from his
correspondence to have been both pleased and amused by the general
success of the work, remarking to his publisher James Fraser a month
after publication that the reviews 'have as yet been all highly favourable', and more than a year later describing the reputation of the sermons as 'exceedingly high in Scotland'.[44] He told Sir Cuthbert Sharpe
that his sermons 'have sold prodigiously' and James Cochrane that
they 'have done exceedingly well and have a very high character both
in Britain and America'. He even jestingly threatened the editor of
Chambers's Edinburgh Journal with a succession of extracts from an inter-
minable sermon as a consequence of his success:

> But as I like to appear in your (to me) most interesting journal
> now and then and am acquiring great celebrity as a writer of
> sermons I send you *a portion* of one which I was thinking like
> Wordsworth in his Excursion of drawing out to an indefinable
> length on the common Courtesies and civilities of life.[45]

With a few notable exceptions modern critics have largely under-
valued, if not ignored, Hogg's *Lay Sermons*. Louis Simpson, however,
does see them as a necessary corrective to the portrait of Hogg in the
'Noctes Ambrosianae' and as a corroboration of his theories of inspiration as reported by contemporaries like R. P. Gillies.[46] Robert Kiely
was the first critic to see the relationship between the *Lay Sermons* and
Hogg's creative work: it illustrates Hogg's development in later life of
'a romantic creed'. Concentrating on the last two sermons, on reviewers and on deistical reformers, he argues that Hogg 'states here and he
demonstrates in his later fiction [...] a belief in a realm of reality differ-

ent from that which can be profitably subjected to rational inquiry', an insight which enriches his subsequent discussion of *The Private Memoirs and Confessions of a Justified Sinner*.[47] David Groves regards *Lay Sermons* within the wider context of the whole body of Hogg's writings, arguing that it provides an explicit treatment of that 'central unifying symbol of the journey' which he believes to be implicit in the majority of Hogg's creative work. He also treats it as a source for establishing Hogg's personal opinions on various subjects.[48] Silvia Mergenthal provides a trenchant and particularly valuable account of the work, foregrounding Hogg's Preface and providing a spirited account of 'Sermon I. Good Principles' and 'Sermon X. Reviewers', analysing them as a vital contribution to Hogg's self-portraiture.[49]

Despite this recent renewal of interest, however, *Lay Sermons* is still a little-known and under-valued Hogg work. This is probably because it has been so inaccessible, never having been reprinted since its original publication in 1834 until now. It undoubtedly deserves more attention than it has received: for its wealth of biographical detail; for its contribution to understanding the Ettrick Shepherd persona both in the 'Noctes Ambrosianae' and in Hogg's own work; for its relationship to Hogg's other writing, to his essays and tales particularly; and insofar as it makes a specific statement of Hogg's own views on original genius and on creative writing. *Lay Sermons* also has a distinctive charm and flavour of its own, being entertaining and readable as well as informative. It is hoped that the present edition, by making the work readily available, may help to establish it as a unique and indispensable aid to a thorough understanding of one of Scotland's major writers.

Notes

1. *Literary Gazette*, 19 April 1834, p.287.
2. 'Regina and her Correspondents', *Fraser's Magazine*, 6 (September 1832), 255-56 (p.255). This article is highly characteristic of William Maginn's *Fraser's* articles, though it is only tentatively attributed to him in *The Wellesley Index to Victorian Periodicals 1824-1900*, edited by Walter E. Houghton and others, 4 vols (Toronto and London: Toronto University Press, 1966-87), II, 334 (hereafter referred to as *Wellesley Index*).
3. See John Galt to Hogg, 6 February 1830, National Library of Scotland (hereafter NLS), MS 2245, fol.156, and Hogg to James Fraser, 14 September 1835, James Hogg Collection, The Beinecke Library, Yale University.
4. See the Introduction to *The Shepherd's Calendar*, ed. by Douglas S. Mack (Edinburgh: Edinburgh University Press, 1995), pp.xiv-xvi.
5. See the Note on the Text to *Tales of the Wars of Montrose*, ed. by Gillian Hughes

(Edinburgh: Edinburgh University Press, 1996), pp.239-45.

6. Hogg to Simeon De Witt Bloodgood, 25 January 1834, Gratz Collection, The Historical Society of Pennsylvania.

7. Hogg to James Fraser, 14 September 1835, James Hogg Collection, The Beinecke Library, Yale University.

8. Hogg to James Fraser, 2 June 1830, James Hogg Collection, The Beinecke Library, Yale University. See the first part of 'The Election of Editor for Fraser's Magazine', *Fraser's Magazine*, 1 (May 1830), 496-508. Hogg applies for the post by letter; this is read out on the hustings by Jerdan, and immediately afterwards Allan Cunningham reads another letter signed 'Mephistophiles'.

9. 'Literary Characters (No.I): James Hogg', *Fraser's Magazine*, 1 (April 1830), 291-300 (pp.292, 298). *Wellesley Index*, II, 321 ascribes the article to Thomas Powell.

10. 'Noctes Bengerianae', *Edinburgh Literary Journal*, 27 December 1828, pp.87-90; 'Noctes Bengerianae. No. II', *Edinburgh Literary Journal*, 21 March 1829, pp.258-60; and 'Dr David Dale's Account of a Grand Aerial Voyage', *Edinburgh Literary Journal*, 23 January 1830, pp.50-54. See Hogg's letter to William Blackwood of 4 January 1830, NLS, MS 4027, fol.178.

11. James Fraser to Hogg, 26 June 1833, NLS, MS 2245, fols.224-25.

12. 'The Shepherd's Noctes, and the reason why they do not appear in Fraser's Magazine', *Fraser's Magazine*, 8 (July 1833), 49-54.

13. Hogg to Peter M'Leod, 25 July 1833, National Museum of Antiquities of Scotland, Edinburgh, OA75 (PSAS VI p.349).

14. James Fraser to Hogg, 18 November 1833, NLS, MS 2245, fol. 234.

15. 'The Cameronian Preacher's Tale', *The Anniversary* (1829), pp.170-91; 'A Tale of Pentland', *The Amulet* (1830), pp.219-41; 'A Lay of the Martyrs', in *A Queer Book*, ed. by P. D. Garside (Edinburgh: Edinburgh University Press, 1995), pp.77-83.

16. Hogg to James Cochrane, 15 June 1835, James Hogg Collection, The Beinecke Library, Yale University.

17. Robert Gilfillan to Hogg, 24 March 1834, NLS, MS 2245, fols.239-40.

18. See the 'Editor's Introduction' to Samuel Taylor Coleridge, *Lay Sermons*, ed. by R. J. White (Princeton and London: Princeton University Press and Routledge & Kegan Paul, 1972), pp.xxix-xxxi (hereafter referred to as Coleridge).

19. This plate precedes 'The Fraserians; or, The Commencement of the year thirty-five. A Fragment', *Fraser's Magazine*, 11 (January 1835), 1-27, and acts as a frontispiece to the relevant volume. Hogg's comment on it is in his letter to James Fraser of 14 September 1835, James Hogg Collection, The Beinecke Library, Yale University.

20. Coleridge, p.238.

21. Coleridge, p.35.

22. Coleridge, p.7.

23. Coleridge, p.34, commented on in the Editor's Introduction, p.xxxvii.

24. Coleridge, p.43.

25. Coleridge, p.131.

26. On seeing large wooded areas in Athol, for instance, Hogg says that he 'wished several times that Dr Johnson had passed that way', in 'A Journey through the Highlands of Scotland, in the months of July and August 1802. Letter IV', *Scots Magazine*, 65 (April 1803), 251-54 (p.253). Compare 'New Year Paper', *The Spy*, No. 19 (5 January 1811), pp.145-51 with Nos. 8, 29, and 71 of *The Rambler*. Hogg's

inclusion of passages from Johnson in his own essays in *The Spy* seems to have been part of a process of testing the sincerity of his literary advisers: this will be examined in more detail in the volume of The Stirling/South Carolina Research Edition of The Collected Works of James Hogg that contains *The Spy*.

27. See, for instance, the following numbers of *The Rambler*: No. 35 (marriage); No. 50 (old age); No. 64 (friendship); No. 148 (parental tyranny); No. 41 (reason and instinct); No. 4 (problems of authorship); No. 93 (on critics and criticism).

28. Silvia Mergenthal, *James Hogg: Selbstbild und Bild: Zur Rezeption des "Ettrick Shepherd"*, Publications of the Scottish Studies Centre of the Johannes Gutenberg Universität Mainz in Germersheim 9 (Frankfurt am Main: Peter Lang, 1990), p.207 (hereafter referred to as Mergenthal). For Mergenthal's further explication of these ideas (in English) see her 'James Hogg's *Lay Sermons* and the Essay Tradition', *Studies in Hogg and his World*, 2 (1991), 64-71.

29. Mergenthal, p.207.

30. 'The Admonition', *The Spy*, No. 44 (29 June 1811), pp.350-52.

31. 'Dreams and Apparitions. Containing George Dobson's Expedition to Hell, and The Souters of Selkirk', in *The Shepherd's Calendar*, ed. by Douglas S. Mack (Edinburgh: Edinburgh University Press, 1995), pp.118-41 (pp.118-19), and 'On the Separate Existence of the Soul', *Fraser's Magazine*, 4 (December 1831), 529-37 (p.529).

32. 'Dogs' and 'General Anecdotes. Sheep', in *The Shepherd's Calendar*, ed. by Douglas S. Mack (Edinburgh: Edinburgh University Press, 1995), pp.57-67 and 94-97 respectively.

33. Mergenthal, pp.211-15.

34. Edward Young, *Conjectures on Original Composition. In a Letter to the Author of Sir Charles Grandison* (London, 1759), p.9 (hereafter referred to as Young).

35. Robert Kiely, *The Romantic Novel in England* (Cambridge, Massachusetts: Harvard University Press, 1972), p.213.

36. *British Critic*, 16 (July 1834), 244.

37. *Monthly Magazine*, 17 (June 1834), 677.

38. *Athenaeum*, 26 April 1834, pp.306-07 (p.306).

39. *Johnstone's Edinburgh Magazine*, 1 (May 1834), 534-38 (pp.535, 537, 538).

40. *Literary Gazette*, 26 April 1834, pp.291-93 (pp. 293, 291, 291).

41. 'Lay Sermons: By the Ettrick Shepherd', *Fraser's Magazine*, 10 (July 1834), 1-10. The compilers of the *Wellesley Index* were obviously deceived by the superficial tone of this review into attributing it to Allan Cunningham (II, 343), whose simple honesty and warm friendship for Hogg would never have permitted him to write it. Maginn, as the effective editor of *Fraser's*, may have hoped to placate John Gibson Lockhart by including this attack on Hogg in the magazine. Lockhart had been incensed by the Glasgow publication in June 1834 of Hogg's anecdotes of Scott, a work which he thought he had been successful in suppressing. In its review of Hogg's anecdotes in the following issue for August 1834 (volume 10, pp.125-56) *Fraser's* would follow the double path of combining overt support for Lockhart with the astute commercial move of reprinting the work in its entirety— this might be supposed to spoil its sales (a move not detrimental to Hogg personally as the Glasgow edition had been pirated from the New York first edition of April) but it would also give the work an increased circulation and therefore militate against Lockhart's wish to suppress it.

42. *Fraser's Magazine*, 10 (July 1834), 1-10 (pp.1-3, 9-10, 4-5, 6, 5).

43. Mrs Garden, *Memorials of James Hogg, the Ettrick Shepherd* (London and Paisley, [n.d.]), pp.309-10.

44. Hogg to James Fraser, 15 May 1834, Gladstone Court Museum, Biggar, BTC31; Hogg to James Fraser, 14 September 1835, James Hogg Collection, The Beinecke Library, Yale University.

45. Hogg to Sir Cuthbert Sharpe, 9 September 1834, NLS, MS 1809, fols.88-89; Hogg to James Cochrane, 8 November 1834, James Hogg Collection, The Beinecke Library, Yale University; undated letter from Hogg to Robert Chambers, NLS, MS 1809, fol.91.

46. Louis Simpson, *James Hogg: A Critical Study* (Edinburgh and London: Oliver & Boyd, 1962), pp.200-01.

47. Robert Kiely, *The Romantic Novel in England* (Cambridge, Massachusetts: Harvard University Press, 1972), pp.208-32 (see particularly pp.211-13 for the discussion of *Lay Sermons*).

48. David Groves, *James Hogg: The Growth of a Writer* (Edinburgh: Scottish Academic Press, 1988), pp.148-51, the quotation being from p.149.

49. Mergenthal, pp.202-15.

A SERIES OF LAY SERMONS

ON GOOD PRINCIPLES

AND GOOD BREEDING

BY THE ETTRICK SHEPHERD

LONDON

JAMES FRASER REGENT STREET

MDCCCXXXIV

TO

Dr. WILLIAM DUNLOP,

THE FOLLOWING

ESSAYS

ARE MOST RESPECTFULLY INSCRIBED

BY HIS ADMIRING FRIEND,

JAMES HOGG.

Preface

IT being likely that after the publication of this volume I shall be called to fill a chair of moral philosophy in some one of the cities of the United States, or Oxford at least; therefore, to prevent disappointment on the one side, and awkwardness on the other, I hereby profess, that a great number of the most valuable maxims and observations in the following work are taken from a MS. translation of the works of an old French monk of the last century, whose name, as the writer of them, or as an author at all, I have never been able to find out in any history or biography.

I have now given so many tales of *perfect truth* to the public, many of them with not one word of truth in them, that I know I shall not be believed in this, and that people will say, "Oho! this is a mere subterfuge of the Shepherd's to get off, in case of any unsound tenets or instances of bad taste." It is, nevertheless, literally true; and I shall tell you how it came to my hand, which was not in a very fair way.

In 1801 I sent a MS. volume of songs, ballads, &c. to a bookseller in Edinburgh (many years since deceased) to publish for me, which he had promised to do. A long time after, he returned a parcel, with a letter, saying the work would not do, and for my own credit he had abstained from publishing it. It was this translation which he returned me, and being greatly chagrined I kept it. I cared not for the loss of my own, for I had it all either in scraps or by heart; so I retained the parcel sent me, which was never more inquired after.

It has now been in my possession for three and thirty years; but there were so many corrections on the margin, and French notes, that I never ventured to look into it till last winter, when I thought I perceived many observations far too valuable to be lost, and I have mixed a part of them up with my own.

JAMES HOGG.

ALTRIVE,
March 31, 1834.

Sermon I

Good Principles

"Why will you bring down my grey hairs with sorrow to the grave?"

MEN and brethren—I address particularly this discourse to my own sex—whether is it better to reflect seriously and frequently on the approaches of old age, or to allow ourselves to be surprised by some remarkable instances of failing, which cannot be disputed? This is a question on which I have often studied, but own to you that I cannot decide it. Frequent and serious meditation on such a subject, one should think, must be very necessary. But then the altered features of old age become agreeable to us by looking at them. We flatter our own grey hairs; and find always such freshness along with our fading, as serves to cherish the opinion, that we are younger than we are, and that we shall live longer than it is possible for us to do.

When I look back on my past life, I see nothing but a vain show through all the space that is past; and when I seriously contemplate the future, I am compelled to believe that the termination of my life is at no great distance. And yet, for all the maxims which I have been able to found on this certain and necessary truth, I cannot say that I think more now of the uncertainty and vanity of life than I did thirty years ago. We are old men before we think much of old age, and are never the first to observe our own decline; nor are the hints given us by our friends exceedingly well received. This is owing, in some degree, to the law of our constitution, which fixes us for a considerable number of years, in the middle period of life, in a state which neither increases nor decays. But it is owing still more to the wisdom of Providence, which has not suffered our relish for life to be destroyed by the certainty of death. Every man has proper seasons for reflection; and, as I am best acquainted with my own thoughts on all subjects, I freely tell you that I have struggled against every suggestion concerning my age; yet I cannot help occasionally stating to myself the probable termination of my life, calculating how many years are likely to elapse before I reach it, and then grasping in my mind the space of as many years which are past. The imaginary period, indeed, is still to come, but I have a standard by which I can measure it; and if I were wise, I might know what it will be. A young man does not possess this advantage. The period of his past life, on which he reflects, is clouded with the ambiguous and uncertain impressions of his infancy. There is something like an eternity that is past hanging on the retrospect. And yet when he takes the whole amount of his life in years, there is a prospect of more to come. With regard to myself, then, I will venture to say, that I was beginning to be an old man as soon as I tried to look forward to the probable termination of my life, and compared it with a fixed number of years already past. I do not desire, however, any one who reads this to apply the rule to himself for finding the beginning of old age. *Bring not down your grey hairs with sorrow to the grave.*

You will naturally ask me, how a man should enjoy the evening of life? Should he marry? By all means. It is the wisest thing he can do. But if he passes forty-five, he should make no unnecessary delay, for he is not far from being old enough. But at any age below sixty, or perhaps seventy, I think his wisest course is to marry; and I shall give you my reasons for it, which I think you will not deny are cogent ones.

You can scarcely call it a failing of old age, but surely one of its concomitants is, to fix our affections more strongly on the persons around us, in proportion as we are about to leave them. We are, perhaps, more susceptible of flattery as we advance in life, or perhaps our age and our weakness together have contracted the circle of our friends. It is, then, the duty of every man to provide against the inconvenience of this secluded state. Let him rear a circle of tender and attached friends around him, who will serve him with affection, and whom he can love without fear. There is joy in the respect paid to you by your countrymen; there is joy in literary or warrior fame; but there is no earthly joy like that of the parent of a virtuous family.

I have had many occasions to see the reverse of this picture, and I confess I never saw it without pity and regret. A solitary stunted tree in the midst of a desert gives you but a faint emblem of it; you see a man who has outlived the pleasures and the uses of living. If he is poor, he is neglected; and if rich, he has reason to suspect every person who approaches him of selfishness. His mercenary hirelings, who counterfeit affection, contrive to banish his real friends. He has no hold of that chain which connects a man with future generations. He has no stimulus to quicken the energies of his mind; and is shut out for ever from the best and only enjoyment of old age, that of his children and grand-children waiting on him with the fondest attention, and never rising up or looking him in the face but to bless him.

Although all the wit and raillery which a certain class of young men employ against the married state were founded in truth and reason, yet they had better enter into it than live on to this unpitied and unprotected stage of existence. That their humour is affected, I can easily believe; for I never knew an instance of such raillery from a man upwards of sixty. Let me advise you, therefore, and I do it most earnestly, to avoid this intemperance, which gives a pledge to your friends against your own happiness, a reason to yourself against entering into that state which will promote it, and which, if you live as long as I have done, and as I wish you to do, you yourself will condemn with unavailing remorse, and *bring down your grey hairs with sorrow to the grave*.

Take a prospect of human life through the vista of reason, and you must perceive that it is a voyage to an undiscovered country. Our provisions wear out, and the vessel turns crazy as we advance. It is a voyage which we have begun, and which we should try to bring to as happy and prosperous a termination as possible. What, then, can we do better than to lay in a good store of provisions, to have honest and true messmates, and with all our skill to steer clear of the quicksands which would swallow us up, and the rocks on which we may be dashed to pieces. With these precautions, Providence for our pilot, and religion for our sheet-anchor, we shall enter the harbour with hope, and look back on the dangers that we have escaped with pleasure and exultation.

There are a number of men, my neighbours and intimate acquaintances, and as good, kind-hearted gentlemen as exist, who, in spite of all that their worthy pastor and I have said to them, still persist in framing objections to the married state. First, they were too young, and their circumstances not sufficiently affluent; then they had some future plan of life which was not matured; then, all at once, they became too old! They now say, it is a melancholy thing to see a man advanced in years with a family about him, whom he can never expect to see settled in the world. But they do not consider that this is melancholy only to the looker-on, not to the man himself. We shall soon be convinced of this, if we consider that we lay as extensive plans, and plant even more trees, both fruit and forest ones, in our old age, than we do in the vigour and prime of youth. The children of an old man give youth and life to his mind; he lives in them, and they hold him, in spite of himself, in connexion with the world, and are a bed of roses to him in his last decline of life. I am far from asserting, with Voltaire, that a family is the sole chance that a man has for immortality; but they certainly give him a chance of living in them until the end of time. I am even grieved to the heart, to see an old favourite tree fall down through decay, and not have one stem springing from its root.

The same temper which makes a man contented with his situation in life, furnishes him with the means of happiness. There is nothing, therefore, more necessary for a man who is approaching the verge of old age, than to cultivate those dispositions of mind which give him friends and cheerfulness at the same time. The rule is easy. Be always more ready to attend to the wants and claims of others, than to exact from them the sacrifices which pride demands. Pride can never bring happiness either in youth or old age. It has an appetite which no respectfulness can satiate, and at the same time a forbidding sourness of aspect that restrains men from giving it the food which it craves. No man can help contemplating the fall of the proud with less compassion than he bestows on the afflicted.

The pleasure of gaining friends is to me the highest of the world. As an old man, I consider myself, on every new accession of this kind, to have touched at some friendly coast, and laid in a fresh stock of necessaries and comforts for my perilous voyage. It is another link added to the chain which attaches me to the world I live in; and as long as I am enabled to gain the affections, and capable of becoming an object of good will to him, I think I am living to some purpose. My own feelings, and the satisfaction of indulging them, convince me of the great use of cultivating benevolent affections, and as much as possible of subduing the tendency in old age to pride and selfishness. A man of an opposite temper complains of the world, when he should complain of himself. His pride is a coat of mail which has defended him against friendship, and his selfishness has become covetousness, merely to give play to his affections. I never yet knew a man capable of making friends in his youth become a miser in his old age. The extraordinary love of money at this stage of life, I have generally found to be a new direction to malevolent passions or licentious enjoyments, which could no longer be indulged. We need not wonder, then, to see old men covetous; but we must pity them when we see them thus *bringing down their grey hairs with sorrow to the grave.*

I have never yet been able properly to understand what Mr. James Russell would call the *otium cum dignitate* of an old man. It is supposed by some, that there is a certain period of life at which we ought to retire from public view, and leave the field open to vigorous and ambitious young men, who will tread the stage with a firmer step, and conduct the business of literature or common life with greater activity. I confess I am beginning to feel this; at least, as far as poetry is concerned; and have given up the field to my younger competitors, with a full dependence on what I have done. Many of my friends will be sorry to read this; but if the revolution of human affairs makes it necessary to retire from a particular situation, it is surely best for such a person to submit quietly to his destiny, and withdraw with a good grace.

Still, I cannot believe there is a given period in every man's life, or in any man's life, at which he should retire from the duties of his station. We have no right to say, that because a man has laboured in an honourable and industrious way for twenty or thirty years, that it is then time for him to sit down and do no more. I object to the position; because there are few who can afford to do it; and, moreover, the habits of industry are painful to give up after being so long accustomed to them. I would, therefore, seriously advise old men to continue on in their accustomed employment, lest *they bring down their grey hairs with sorrow to the grave.*

I do not deny that many old men are jostled from the active scenes of life by the impetuosity of young men, who are eager to occupy their stations. But when this happens it is a misfortune, not a privilege; and it is a man's duty to defend himself, by every just method, against any such encroachments made upon him. The difficulty, no doubt, is increased when the station requires activity and diligence more than experience and wisdom; yet, in most of the instances of this kind which I have witnessed, and been at the trouble to examine, I have found the blame to be more in the weakness of the man than the infirmities of his age.

I do not at all consider old age to be such a state of helpless depression of the powers of the mind as it is generally supposed to be; and I beg that you will attend to this in the latter stage of life, as it may be of some use to you. We are not fond of acknowledging the infirmities really connected with old age, and we are very old men before we will allow that age is the cause of our failing. In other distresses of life we accept the sympathy of our friends, because our vigour may be restored; but in old age we are often hurt by their sympathy, because the disease is incurable. When we are convicted of any of the undeniable marks of age, as wrinkles, grey hairs, or defect of sight, it is both laughable and pitiable to hear every one asserting that these are not the marks of age in his case, as he had had them all since he was thirty!

It is a pity that any one should indulge in such ingenious delusions; for it is our bounden duty to accustom ourselves to the thoughts of the very rapid approach either of death or old age. I have no objections to the conceit that we are extremely vigorous for our years; but let us, at all events, be convinced that old age and death are fast approaching, and let us be prepared for either. We know, to a certainty, that we must all shortly follow one another into the dark and silent mansions of the grave; but, blessed be God, we have also the prospect of following one another into the regions of eternal happiness!

I therefore conceive that the best species of discipline for these great changes, is to subject our minds, as well as our bodies, to vigorous exercises as long as we are able; for I am certain that exercise and temperance preserve the body in a sound state; and equally certain, that delightful study, the exercise of the mind, gives full vigour to its powers until extreme old age. It is rare that a studious man outlives his faculties, unless these faculties have been very rath in their growth; for precocity of talent never abides till old age. Providence by this seems to afford us a proof of the vanity of all human acquirements, by giving an extraordinary display of mental exertions at one period of life, and taking them away at another.

At all events, there is one fact, which I think my limited knowledge of the world warrants me in asserting. It is, that in proportion as we improve the powers of our mind, we shall retain them for a shorter or longer period. I have always found a greater number of old men of sound and vigorous minds engaged in the professions which require thought, than in those which require little mental exertion. Perhaps something may be deducted for the original strength and turn of mind which fitted them for their profession: but I do not allow much for this; as I am firmly persuaded that no man can know what length he is able to proceed in literary pursuits, or in a liberal profession, till he makes the trial. Genius, or what may be called a peculiar fitness of mind, will certainly lead one man to a greater height of excellence than another; but it does not follow that our single talent may not be in a state of improvement till the very end of life.

Consider, then, that it must be of vast importance to those who are verging towards the period of old age, to be able to lay hold of something within themselves which they can carry along with them—something which will be a resource and comfort to them under the languor and tediousness of life's decay. The reflection of a life spent in just and honourable actions is a source of very great comfort in old age; but God has not formed man to derive his sole happiness, in any stage of life, either from meditating on the past, or anticipating the future. The most peevish old men I have ever known were such as had earned fame by some insulated action, and who had nothing else to depend on. They were obliged to draw constantly from the same stock, till the world began to conceive that they were bankrupt, and they were daily disappointed in the respect to which they thought themselves entitled. Be assured, therefore, that a happy and respectable old age must have something to shew as well as to relate. We must see what the men are, as well as hear what they have been. I know nothing better, then, under the sun, than still to be doing with our hand what our hand findeth to do, and always to be busily employed in such work as suits our years, even when we are approaching the last bourn of all the human race, beyond which there is neither knowledge nor device; and by persevering in this, none of us *shall bring down our grey hairs with sorrow to the grave.*

It is not to be expected that a man labouring under a load of years, and constantly shewing that he is unable to bear it, can be a good companion to the young, the giddy, and the volatile. It is in vain to look for sympathy or respect where there is so much dissimilarity both in temper and years. We old men look on the actions of the young as foolish, and their pursuits as frivolous; while they consider our maxims as tinctured more with the peevishness than the wisdom of age. For this very reason I like to make friends and companions of those who are forty years my juniors. I thus renew the youth of my mind, and have attachments growing upon me as my old friends drop away. I try to make young men be in love with old age before they arrive at it, and shew them that happiness and hilarity are not confined to the young. I also find many occasions of infusing the experience of age under the guise of equality; for, unless piqued by insolence or vulgarity, I never in conversation set myself above the humblest individual.

After all, I do not see why young people should not be entertained, nor do I believe they are at all incapable of being entertained, with the conversation and gaiety of an old man. When I make them forget my age, I forget it also myself. I account it an essential duty, and I am sure it is a source of great happiness, to break down, as much as possible, the jealousies which are apt to subsist between the young and the old. They are afraid of our peevishness, and we are afraid of their frivolity. But let us always be satisfied that we meet on equal terms, and then they will love our cheerfulness, they will be flattered by our attentions, they will attain at an easy rate the experience which has cost us dear, and perhaps acquire a more sedate and manly character by the apothegms of age.

I advise every man advanced in age, therefore, to begin now and continue on, however old, this happy expedient of stepping back to the scenes which you have left, and mingling occasionally with the enchanting circles of innocence and youth, especially if you have any thing in your countenance or manners which invites all the young people of the families in which you visit to flock about you, hang about you, and use every familiarity with you. This is delightful, and an infallibly good sign of an old man; for it is a curious fact, that children are the best judges of character at first sight in the world.

There is an old Scots proverb, "They're never cannie that dogs an' bairns dinna like;" and there is not a more true one in the whole collection. "Let no such man be trusted."

No man needs to fear the tediousness and insipidity of old age, provided his soul be kept in proper subjection to the will of his Creator. I am often surprised at seeing decent, respectable old men incessantly amused with trifling games, repeated almost in the same manner for a thousand times. I am addicted to some of these myself; but at that I do not wonder; for there is a principle in my constitution that requires constant excitement.

The book of nature, and especially those pages of it in which the human mind is delineated in its various attitudes and exertions, is the choicest study of man at any period of his life. It is good for us to know ourselves; but the minds of other men are a sort of mirror which reflects our own image; and you will always find, that as you know other men more, you will be the better acquainted with yourself. Add to this, that when we have advanced to a certain period of life, our minds may be grown to their full size; and though we do our best in retaining and polishing what we have collected, or in substituting the results of the understanding in the room of the force and play of the fancy, yet we must confess that, with respect to some powers of our mind, we are a little on the decline. In this stage, if a man seclude himself wholly from the world, his understanding will grow rigid, his philosophy antiquated, and his maxims and expressions quite unfashionable. Let us, then, live in the world while we are in it; for it is better to keep pace with the times; and, since we have always one door by which we can return to the world, why shut it against ourselves for ever?

Old men generally complain of the difficulty of making new friends: this is a great calamity, as it happens at a time when their old companions are daily disappearing, and when they are most in need of a succession of new ones. Perhaps, too, there may often be a little selfishness in this complaint, as the deaths of our contemporaries is a warning to ourselves. I know, indeed, of no friendship stronger than that which has grown with our years, and brings up in its associations all the fond recollections of our infancy and youth. But we must submit to such a separation; and philosophy can give us no wiser instruction than that which teaches us to gain the love and respect of others, when we lose those who are dear and valuable. Providence has also, in our transitory state, wisely contrived a remedy for this disease of old age, if we choose, when we are young men, to avail ourselves of it. We may so connect ourselves with the world as to have the fair prospect of dear and tender relations to fill the place of our departed friends, and to come with claims on us which will keep alive the best feelings of our nature, and excite our exertions and industry to the last period of our lives. This, with the fear of God always before our eyes, and a humble confidence in his mercy, will keep our old hearts perfectly at ease, and our grey hairs shall sink down into the grave in peace.

But of this we may rest assured, that there is no period of this life free from its peculiar cares and distresses. There is a portion of calamity alloted to men in all the stages of this probationary journey—this first stage on the road of immortality. When we contemplate old age at a distance, and see our seniors tottering under its burdens and cares, we are apt to say they have a double portion; but we suppose many things in their situation which they do not feel; we paint the distress of old age with the vigour and fancy of youth. Does any one believe that an old man thinks of the shortness and uncertainty of his few remaining years with as much seriousness as his friends around him? It is quite the contrary. The hope of life is increased with our weakness, and that hope is never extinguished until the bitterness of death is past. Death is less feared as we proceed in the voyage, until a certain age, when we get much more frightened and careful of ourselves than the young are. Still death does not appear to come any nigher to our doors, which is another wise provision of Providence for man's earthly happiness; and the truth is, that in this precarious state of existence the danger is nearly equal to us all. Providence has given us blessings peculiar to every period of life; and there is no stage of our existence in which the real calamities of life are more concealed from our view, or less felt, than in old age.

My design in all this is to reconcile my younger brethren of the human race to a state to which they are all fast approaching, and which appears terrible to them only because they have no experience of it. But while I unveil the mysteries of our comfort, I would by no means paint old age as absolutely a state of rest from the cares of life, or as bringing certain and unmixed happiness to all who arrive at it. It is enough if I convince you that it is not what it seems to be. Were I to do more, I might carry you to the utmost verge of life with the idea of happiness which you could never obtain, whilst I did not prepare you for what you may enjoy.

Remember, then, that your pursuits in the vigour of life determine, in almost all cases, the happiness of your declining years. A man may be old without health, or wisdom, or independence, or friends; and when he is so he will not easily procure those blessings.

It is only by regular exercise and temperance that a man can acquire that constitution that will wear off the depredations of time to the last. By daily additions to his knowledge he will acquire that strength of mind which will give the full possession of his stores for a long time after he is incapable of increasing them. He has to guard against being overtaken with old age and with want at the same time; and surely if God shall enable him to advance farther into the vale of years than his companions who began the journey with him, there is no harm in his cherishing those dispositions of mind which will gain him the respect and good-will of those who set out a few years after him. Let every man attend to these instructions, if he wishes to attain a happy old age; and if he chooses to obey them he will have the advantage of enjoying more happiness from this day forward than he can have by following any other course. A vigorous constitution, strength of mind, and agree-able manners, not only make old age comfortable, but in the acquisi-tion of them a man has infinitely higher satisfaction than is ever dreamed of by the effeminate and licentious part of mankind. An old man of this character appreciates full well the common maxim, that virtue is its own reward. He looks back on the sunshine of a well-spent life, and feels the advantage of his temperance and virtues in the health of body and soundness of mind which he enjoys.

If we are at no pains to prepare ourselves for advanced years, we are in danger of growing insipid, and of being neglected at that period of life when soothing and attention are most necessary. We see many instances of men outliving their usefulness, neglected by their friends, and complaining bitterly of that neglect. This will ever happen when the disease of old age is not endured with meekness and cheerfulness. Let us not demand the sympathy of the world for a disease of which there is no hope, but let us at all events endeavour to deserve their admiration and love; for *why should you bring down your grey hairs with sorrow to the grave?*

I know you will say, long before reaching this point, that this man of the mountains is unequal to the task he has assumed; for what knows he of life or manners? You are wrong: we shepherds find

> "Tongues in trees, books in the running brooks,
> Sermons in stones, and good in every thing."

And were it not that a dear and esteemed friend is at the head of moral philosophy in this country, I could so exhaust the subject that it should no more be taken up or handled here or elsewhere; and I shall con-clude this discourse by one potent piece of advice, which will convince every person who reads it how well I see into human nature; and it is this:

Above all things on earth avoid the error too common of giving up your fortune, and the necessary independence of your character, till you part with your life. Let no misplaced love to your dearest friends, nor even to your children, prevail on you to do this; else you shall assuredly shed the tear and rue the deed. It is better to be deceived by the flattering attentions of those who expect something from you, than to be neglected by those who think you past the use of living. Old men are often deceived into this conduct by their fondness and folly, and it never fails to embitter their remaining days. They absurdly imagine that affection pulls as strongly on the side of youth as on that of age; and nothing can convince them of the law of nature on this point except the trial. I adjure every man, especially such whose means of subsistence and exertions are linked together, never to give up his power of superintendency and direction as long as he is able to act, even though not with his usual vigour. Unless from severe sickness or mental derangement, I cannot suppose any person unfit to direct the business of his own family; why, then, should he reduce himself to a situation in which he may be jealous of encroachment, or in which those about him may think that he is so. The man who does this is sure to *bring down his grey hairs with sorrow to the grave*.

Sermon II

Young Women

"Because the daughters of Zion are haughty, and walk with stretched-forth necks and wanton eyes, walking and mincing as they go, and making a tinkling with their feet. * * * In that day the Lord will take away the bravery of their tinkling ornaments about their feet, and their cauls and their round tires like the moon, the chains, and the bracelets, and the mufflers, the bonnets, and the ornaments of the legs, and the headbands, and the tablets, and the ear-rings, the rings, and the nose-jewels, the changeable suits of apparel, and the mantles, and the wimples, and the crisping-pins, the glasses, and the fine linen, and the hoods, and the vails."

THIS is a most extraordinary enumeration of our evangelical prophet's. I have always thought that the present age over-topped all former ones in emulation for fine dresses and ornaments of every description; but I have been wrong; for what are the most splendid dresses in Europe compared with those of the Hebrew ladies? Isaiah was a shepherd, and the son of a shepherd; but, like others of his class, he has had an eye to the comely daughters of his people, and, as appears from other parts of his writings, noted well both what was becoming and what was ridiculous. I shall therefore take advantage of the prophet's description of the fantastic dresses of the daughters of Jerusalem to point out a few failings in the characters of my beloved young countrywomen, and recommend some duties which, if they attend to, they will be the better and happier as long as they live. I know they will smile at this presumption, and say one to another that age has not cured the shepherd of his inherent vanity. But they should remember, that my years and separation from the world give me a right not only to speak my mind freely to the young and giddy, but also the power of looking at the charms of the loveliest of women with a steadier and more discriminating eye than those can do who are overpowered with them and flatter them. I by that means possess a darkened glass through which I can look at the sun without being dazzled by the beams which conceal his dark spots. At all events, what is so well meant can never be taken amiss.

I must begin by disclosing to you the main fountain from whence all your errors and failings derive their source: it is a false and defective education. It is peculiarly unfortunate for you that at an early period of life the qualities which make you agreeable are quite of a different kind from those which are afterwards necessary to the discharge of your most important duties. The period of the few years between the girl and the woman is the most important one of your whole life: it is that period which frequently gives the character its peculiar tone and bias; for though you are prohibited, by the custom of the world, from acting a shining part, yet you have room to indulge in the liveliness which ends in the various arts which end in coquetry, or in the frivolity which ends in nothing. You dare not even let the little genuine information you have appear, for you know it would be regarded as affectation.

In short, your whole mode of education is unpropitious to future happiness. You are called to act a new part before you can possibly have secured one of the necessary qualifications for it; and at the same time there is something in the giddiness of seventeen which promises you approbation, though you may not deserve it. If a blunt man may use a plain expression to you, it is owing to the attentions of this important period that we find so many beautiful and agreeable women more ignorant than they should be. Their power of pleasing begins at an early age, and they cultivate no other acquirements than those by which they made their first approaches to estimation. The approbation of the world is all that they value; and the only difference between the girl and the woman is a little difference in stature, and perhaps comeliness of form.

Now I appeal to yourselves if this frivolous mode of education is either preparing you for happiness in this life or that which is to come? The sole motive inculcated on a young woman, and that exclusive of all others, is that she shall make herself acceptable and agreeable to the circle around her. Her happiness and success in life are represented to her as depending more on the power of pleasing than any other qualification, not excepting the approbation of the wise and the good. Consequently she becomes agreeable more than prudent, and possesses a greater command of temper than exercise of understanding; and, what is more, this notorious defect in education has more influence on beautiful women than on those of a more ordinary appearance. The former are more exposed to those attentions and flatteries which destroy them, and the latter enjoy the important advantage of applying their minds at an early period to those studies which the others cannot have time to think of until they are incapable of pursuing them. A few young women of prudence and foresight will occasionally attend to those concerns fitting them for the duties of a wife and mother, but, alas, how few! Now, consider with yourselves how a man could build a house, make a coat or a pair of shoes, without ever having tried it before. What a bungling business he would make of either! you will say. A hundred for one of you in the higher ranks of life place yourselves in the same situation the first fair opportunity that offers.

My purpose now is to address such young women who, in consequence of fine persons and engaging manners, are in the greatest danger in their progress through early life. I am so much afraid of flattery and vanity combined, that I never see a beautiful young lady exposed to them, that I am not in pain for her lest they should triumph over her prudence and understanding. Let such take warning. A prudent general should be on his guard, although danger is not apparent.

I shall suppose you, then, accustomed from your infancy to yield implicit obedience to the best of mothers, and to listen to her as to an oracle of undisputed authority; that she has had the art of forming the minds of her children to submission, without laying them under any restraint. If so, then you can probably hear the voice of approbation without having your vanity excited; but be not too sure, nor rashly conclude that you are so fully prepared as to be in no danger. It is much better to possess an inclination for further knowledge than that liveliness of disposition which expresses every thing. There is an ingenuous frankness which I am far from condemning, which consists simply in shewing the mind as it is. It is the purity which has nothing to conceal, nothing to be ashamed of, nothing to counterfeit, and nothing to affect. This frankness in your tender and confiding sex is most amiable; but I request you to observe the difference between this charming frankness and that slight and petulant imitation of it which some girls affect, and remind one of the language of statesmen who boast of apparent openness while they have something material to conceal.

The frankness, then, which I recommend to you is that which displays your whole soul and character to every person you converse with. It must be a chastened and intelligent frankness which makes it manifest that reserve would injure you. Be free, therefore, in all your conversation, whether with your friends or with strangers, not only because you have nothing to conceal, but because you have always something to learn from them. I am decidedly averse to all that assumed superiority of address which obliges a lady to shift her character, and act a part suited to the company in which she is placed. It is often not very easy to overcome this; and I have seen most sensible and accomplished young ladies terribly curbed and kept down by it. There is nothing for it but frankness and vivacity, which in a young lady will put down every stately barrier. Nothing great is expected from her, which makes her little sallies the more pleasant; and such a picture of happy cheerfulness cannot fail to be reflected even from the breast of a cynic. It is like music at a feast—the effect is so pleasing, although not lasting; it is a sweet fragrance on a passing breeze—a savour of delight, which cheers and amends the heart.

On the other hand, liveliness without an improved understanding may place you in very dangerous circumstances. If you are mistress of one or two agreeable qualities, they expose you to constant flattery, which, if your strength of mind be not thoroughly able to resist, the consequences may be pernicious in the extreme. In such a case, your whole fortune of charms is in ready money, wholly at your own disposal, and soon expended. The vanity and presumption of beauty and youth persuade you that it is unnecessary to add to your stock. You thus pass onward to the sober duties of life with the petulance of girlish vivacity, and are sure to render yourself despised and neglected when the effect of your transitory arts of pleasing is no more.

It is hardly possible for one of my retired habits and sequestered life to point out the very path you should follow, from your childhood up; but I have been a close observer of nature for the few chances I have had, and I have always observed that in your case much, much indeed, depends on the mother, which leads to a laxity of education from one generation to another. What, for instance, can be more pernicious to young women than that their education should be so often conducted without an object? They are compelled to attend to a course of flimsy studies which serve to dissipate their minds, and which can never be brought to any use in the future part of their lives. This, it is true, may partly be attributed to the conditions imposed on your sex, which prevent you from entering into any profession which requires great activity or deep learning; and because you have little to do in the active scenes of life, it is, I suppose, understood that you have as little to learn. I must now address you, for a single sentence, in the abstract.

At seventeen the education of a lady is thought to be complete. Let us consider what she has then attained. She can speak and even read the language of her country with grace and propriety; she has French and Italian—of what sort? only a few smatterings, to which the natural sweetness of her voice gives a prettiness as she recites the few sentences, or sings the few verses, of which she is mistress. She is taught to have command of all the most agreeable smiles; and her natural liveliness and flippancy are sometimes carefully adorned with something like sentiment. O, how delightful and how killing that is! Then the attitudes! What is to become of the hearts of all mankind? Ah, those are so graceful, so insinuating!—and which, added to the elegance of the dress, make the dear creatures quite irresistible. Thus prepared, she is introduced into company to carry all before her by a *coup de main*.

Now, this is a true picture; you cannot deny it. But, my dear girls, consider the matter seriously. If you enter the field with such sanguinary designs, you rush into a scene of the utmost danger, and engage in a warfare where you must either speedily conquer or never. You employ only weapons which must do all their execution at the first onset. Time blunts them, and experience will not enable you to use them with more success; and then, should your enemy yield at discretion, are you sure that the arms which conquered him will keep him in subjection? I fear not. Something more substantial is wanting. You may gain the sanguine heart of a youthful lover by your outward graces, but it is only the soul within that can retain him.

These are subjects the consideration of which is of infinite consequence; and in attending to them as you ought to do, you will have occasion to improve your understanding, to regulate your temper, and increase your humility. In the practice of virtues which will equally secure your respectability and your happiness, you will find objects worthy of your choice, and greatly preferable to the talent of exciting the envy of weak women, or the admiration of insipid and volatile men.

It is grievous to see a superior mind dissipated by the conversation of those who affect liveliness because they are deficient in understanding. The great majority of the fashionable female world are in this condition at a certain time of life; and it is difficult for any young lady of the same rank to escape the contamination. She is apt to become enamoured with manners which are apparently amiable and engaging, and which cost her little expense or trouble to acquire, and her mind is insensibly weakened by imitation.

I do not advise you, my young countrywomen, to fly from the world, but I earnestly recommend it to your particular attention, never to allow your minds to sink below the tone and vigour which mark their natural strength. Be as gay and playful if you will as those who assume gaiety to conceal their weakness, but never cease at any period of life to increase your knowledge, and, by exercise, to improve the powers of your understanding.

Having now warned you to beware of the flippancy of your female associates, and of those who make liveliness compensate for the defects of their understanding, I must next give you a few hints concerning the books which you ought and ought not to peruse. The means of improvement in regard to your sex are chiefly reading and conversation. The first gives you knowledge, and the latter teaches you how to use it; and much circumspection is requisite in both cases. Now, I must confess that I am seldom pleased with the books which I see in the hands of young ladies whom I esteem and for whose well-being I am anxious. These circulating libraries are ruin for you, as from them you get so much that is nothing but froth and fume. I can never help being pleased when I see one of my own volumes in a young lady's hand whom I like, and yet I cannot say very much for them either; only thus much I can say, that these dreamy stories about ghosts and apparitions and persecutions are not half so apt to poison the mind as those of another class which I shall describe. Ladies' novels, for instance, with the exception only of those of two at present living, are all composed in a false taste, and at the same time convey so little instruction, that it would be better for you never to open them. What benefit can a young mind receive from contemplating scenes which, though interesting, have neither nature nor probability to recommend them? You may see, perhaps, virtue rewarded and vice punished; but while these necessary acts of justice are painted, you see nothing of the reality of life, none of the characters with which you are acquainted; and it is far from being a safe amusement for young ladies to have their feelings and imaginations wrought upon by the fictions of romance, even though the book should hold up nothing but the fairest sides of fair characters. The mind by these is apt to become too highly toned for the common incidents of life; and the readers of such works are apt to be wound up to such a pitch as to be precisely like those who never enjoy themselves save when they are under the influence of intoxication.

Another bad thing in these books is, that they always bring virtue into trying and critical situations, so that you must have the delineation of vice along with the other,—all its modes of attack, and the most insinuating infusion of its poison. Vice cannot be exhibited in detestable colours when the intention of the author is to make resistance meritorious. Where there is no allurement, there is no temptation; and it too frequently happens that the worst character in the piece is the most engaging. It is even uniformly so with the greatest and most accomplished novelist that ever was born; and hence, in the mind of a young reader especially, all the distinctions between virtue and vice are broken down. Think, then, what mischief may be wrought in a youthful female mind by such pernicious representations of character. If the agreeable but wicked hero of the piece be reformed, there is a dangerous desire excited to make proselytes; and if he be punished, the tears which should have been shed for his guilt fall for the misfortunes of the guilty. I recommend, therefore, to your attention those works which give a real picture of such characters as have existed in the world, and do exist, both for your profit and amusement; for whenever your author loses sight of nature and probability, you lose all hold of him and interest in his work.

It is good to indulge in reading history; for though the incidents are often surprising, and such as one durst not exhibit in a novel, and likewise many of the characters above the capacity of ordinary readers to comprehend, it nevertheless has this to recommend it, that it gives a faithful and true picture of the passions which have agitated mankind, and the events which have resulted therefrom in real life, especially from the ambition of princes and the selfish intrigues of courtiers and flatterers. But in history, though we often see vice successful, it is never amiable; and, from the nature of its composition, and the greatness of its objects, the series of events, the dignity of the actors, and the issue of all worldly events, which it does and must exhibit, you will review lessons on human affairs well calculated to promote your knowledge and humility. There you see the rapid decay of all worldly grandeur, beauty, and ambition; so that the whole of history, to a contemplative mind, is one huge *memento mori* – a good lesson still to keep before your eyes.

Romances, on the other hand, give a transient and false view of human life; the figures are overcharged with colouring, the whole is intended to please, and there is nothing in the background to teach us that all is vanity. The personages of romance are indeed conducted through most difficult and distressing scenes; their virtue is exposed to the greatest risks, while the art of the author must, at all events, preserve it from contamination. Many delicate sentiments may be introduced, and much heroic love displayed, and, when you least expect it, the seas, and interventions of all sorts, which a little while before seemed altogether insurmountable, disappear at once; the stratagems of rivals, and the opposition of parents, are all exhausted; and the marriage of the hero and heroine closes the grand outrageous fiction.

Some of these works may be exceedingly amusing to you, though I confess they never were so to me; but I maintain, that if you read such books, you will never be instructed. What are regarded as fine sentiments are of no use if arising out of unnatural and improbable adventures; and I farther assure you, on the credit of a poet, that I never knew a young lady the better of her reading when she read for excitement alone. Never expect to be deceived into wisdom, nor to find it when you are not in direct search of it. The road lies through thickets of briers and thorns, and there are some steep ascents by the way of so hazardous a nature, that you require some resolution to carry you forward. But if you come immediately into meadows of flowers, and follow the endless meandering of beautiful rivers, you have reason to fear that you have mistaken the road. But forget not this, that "wisdom is the principal thing: therefore get wisdom, and with all thy gettings get understanding." But in proving this, I might quote one half of the Proverbs of Solomon.

I entreat you, then, to read such books as may instruct more than amuse you. Accustom yourself to receive pleasure from the taste and good sense of the author, more than from the incidents he relates. Admire the thoughts which paint to you what you yourself should be, more than those which give you the possible situation of others; and, above all, permit me seriously to advise you to read those books only which are recommended and selected by those who have your well-being at heart, and never by those who may have any interest or selfish purpose in misleading you. It can be no reproach to you, that in the vast number of books within your reach, neither your years nor experience enable you to make the most prudent choice. At no period of life is it safe to read a multitude of miscellaneous works; therefore you will act wisely, if you endeavour, by the advice of parents, pastors, or preceptors, to form your taste, so that you may be qualified for making your own selection before you become sole mistress of your actions.

It will be more useful for you to understand what you read than to remember it. Your mind may treasure up many things relating to useful knowledge by the aid of memory; but I would prefer that exercise of the understanding, which, if well improved, makes us master of the thoughts of the author, which enables us to relish them, and to see their full force and beauty as we go along. This exercise of the understanding is of great value. It is acquired by attention to what you read, much more than by reading a great deal, and it gives you the power on all occasions of drawing from your own stock, instead of detailing the detached and ill-sorted opinions of others, from a memory which cannot be at all times correct. I know nothing of greater importance to a young woman than the power of thinking for herself. If your understanding be not disciplined to the task, it behoves you to strengthen it by making it act with precision and force on every book you read. If you derive no other advantage from this, it will at least keep you from quoting your father or your mother, or more probably Lord Byron or Anacreon Moore, as authorities for such wayward sentences as you may chance to detail from memory.

The same management and discretion of mind may be still more usefully employed in company; for you may always consider conversation as an extemporary book, wherein, without much order or method, you may read the wit and common sense of your neighbours. It is a collection from many authors of delicate humour, of serious reflections, of interesting anecdotes, and sometimes of little narratives of common and domestic events. The art lies in mixing the ingredients in such a manner as to make each individual believe his taste has been consulted in the composition. Every person has a right to be satisfied with what he hears in the company of his friends, provided it be the sincere desire of the speaker to please every individual by what he says. I need not inform you, however, that there is a period of life at which a young lady may appear to be supposed too much in the light, if she shall force her sentiments into the current of general conversation. When they are perfectly correct, and even well-timed, there may still be a deficiency of that reserve and diffidence which should have taught her not to utter them. You will be able to judge of this by the forced complaisance, and sometimes silence, of your hearers; and you may lay it down as a general rule, that it is always time for you to cease speaking, when those you wish to please seem no longer disposed to listen to you.

Youth imposes this restraint on you, and during that period you may feel the inconvenience of it, and be ready to envy and blame those who have got the ear of the world for depriving you of the exercise of your tongue. But, depend on it, it is the safest course for you to listen more than speak; it is so easy for young persons in their inexperience to go wrong, if they indulge themselves too much in speaking in company. The liveliness of your imagination may so easily mislead your judgment, that you may acquire the habit of connecting sentences without that precise connexion of thought which is essential to good conversation, and may go on to the end of your life tiring your companions with common place observations, merely because you were taught to speak, before you were able to understand. I do not retract what I have formerly said to you concerning that open frankness which is so becoming in every character and at every period of life; but I request you to consider, that this frankness consists in having nothing to conceal, not in uttering sentiments incongruous to your years, or inconsistent with good sense and an improved understanding.

I have often noted, that young ladies endeavour to shine in conversation long before they are capable of making themselves agreeable in mixed company of all ages. They are often compelled to make a bold stroke, and expose some striking peculiarity, which is far from being the most congenial quality of their young minds. It is not, perhaps, unsuitable to the gay moments of social intercourse to intersperse something of the ludicrous; and there are some characters who may be considered as a seasoning to the feast of conversation; but by no means rest your introduction to good company on the display of any oddity, however agreeable you may suppose it to be to them. In early life it is unsafe to indulge in the ludicrous of any sort, until you have won by the gentleness, innocence, and simplicity of your character. You must be beloved for your good qualities, before you attempt to be admired for your shining ones.

If you attend to these particulars, delivered to you in sincerity and love, your qualities will be of such a nature as to make you estimable in any situation or in any company. Gentleness and modesty are equally attractive to the high and the low, to the learned and the unlearned. In possessing what is unassuming and amiable, you interfere with no person's claims, and you interrupt the progress of no person's vanity. You secure the silence of the severe, and the approbation of the worthy. Be assured, then, that you may make yourself very agreeable to your friends and associates, although you are not too eager, on your entrance into life, of displaying the shining qualities you possess. I have seen teasing and disagreeable effects produced by the ambition of young people to shine where they should have been listening for instruction. Sometimes they acquire a degree of irrecoverable petulance by the easy victories which they obtain over modest merit. Depend on it, every wise person feels sensibly disappointed when the vanity or forwardness of a young, inexperienced person of either sex deprives him of the instructions of the learned or gifted. What is still more serious, this petulance becomes incorrigible; the reward of it also is sure to be the reserve of your friends, and the ultimate consequence is likely to be an exclusion from every select meeting where people meet to enjoy free and rational conversation. Be it your great care, then, always to bring your share of information and good sense to the feast of reason, which, accompanied with modesty, will insure you a welcome reception, and the approbation of the wise and good.

Keep this, then, in remembrance, that in conversation, as in reading, you must raise your understanding to be equal to what you hear. Use your endeavour to have that distinct perception of every sentence uttered in company, which will give your mind the precise idea of the person who uttered it. A quick apprehension will make you a more agreeable companion than a smart reply. That little degree of vanity which enters into the composition of every man of learning and genius, however modest, is more flattered by being distinctly understood than well answered. Avoid, therefore, that disagreeable absence of manner and vacancy of countenance, when you listen to your seniors; for they are the indications of a weak and conceited mind. Shew, at least, that desire to understand them, which will make them adapt their observations to your capacity. If you wish to please your friends by your conversation, you must first learn to be pleased with theirs. Never allow yourself to be hurried away by the dangerous desire of speaking when you ought to be silent; but remember, there is an eloquent silence which displays the intelligence as well as the modesty of a young lady. First improve your mind, and then display its powers.

I have indited nothing as yet to you regarding your religious duties, and shall do it very shortly. My first great injunction, then, is, KEEP THE SABBATH. Do not be seen flying about with gentlemen in gigs and carriages, nor walking and giggling in the fields; for such behaviour is lightsome, and highly disreputable. Attend Divine service once every Sunday at least, even though your minister should be *a bore*, as too many of them are, repeating the same monotonous sentences from day to day, and from year to year. Still, it is your duty to attend Divine worship, to join in praise and prayer with the community of Christians to whom you belong, and listen, reverently and attentively, to the word preached, as you know not whence a blessing may come, or when it may light.

But as the attendance on Divine service takes up but a small portion of the day, in directing your studies for the remainder of it I am rather at a loss. I cannot insist on your reading of sermons, not even my own, for I never could do it myself, except Sterne's and Boston's, the two greatest opposites in nature. The BIBLE is by far the most inexhaustible book in the world, even laying aside its Divine origin altogether. For its great antiquity, simplicity of narrative, splendour of poetry, and wise and holy injunctions, there is no work once to be compared with it; therefore, by all means, read your Bible, and attend to all the ordinances of Christianity; for it is beautiful and becoming to see a young person attending reverently upon these, and can scarcely fail to make her more acceptable both with God and man. Therefore attend diligently on the ordinances of religion, and read your Bible,–all save the book of Leviticus, which I always make my own children leave out. The study of the Jewish ceremonial law can be of no benefit to any one, but least of all to a young lady. I wish that book had been cancelled from the Holy Scriptures; for there are many of the injunctions so disgusting, that they cannot be read even by men.

I believe I may be singular in this idea, but I have always thought it would be best for young women to read the New Testament before the Old one. In youth, their minds are like wax softened by the fire, and ready to take any impression; and surely the Gospels, containing the pure, unblamable, and holy life of our Saviour, his love for our fallen race, sufferings, death, and resurrection, must leave an impression on their tender minds never to be effaced. They can then read the history of the Jews, and the prophecies concerning Him who was to come afterwards, and wonder at their precise and extraordinary fulfilment.

In attendance on all the ordinances of religion, be sure that your dress be plain and modest. Avoid by all means such ridiculous ornaments as the prophet describes at the beginning of this essay. Lay these aside for balls and assemblies, and there dazzle as much as you like; but in the house of God let always modesty of carriage, and decency of deportment and dress, prevail. I shall conclude this address with the beautiful advice of the wise man, "Remember now thy Creator in the days of thy youth."

Sermon III

Good Breeding

"A wholesome tongue is a tree of life; but perverseness therein is a
breach in the spirit."

WHEN the great moral philosopher of Israel dictated this, it is evident
that he alluded to our daily conversation; one of those constant mental ingredients which contribute so much to the happiness or misery of
a family or community. I shall therefore dedicate this discourse solely
to the best means of improving ourselves in that, the most useful of all
accomplishments.

The first rule, then, in conversation is to please the people with
whom it is your lot to converse. This to a young person appears a
much more difficult task than it really is. At the period of life at which
I write this, and I have many brethren of mankind of the same age, or
thereabouts, we think the young are more agreeable when they discover an ingenuous and modest disposition, than when they endeavour to display the powers of their understanding. It frequently happens, however, in both sexes, during the period between youth and
maturity, that there is a strong desire to speak, where the previous
desire of pleasing has not been attended to. I have seen many young
men positively dogmatical, when they ought to have been receiving
instruction. But it should be considered, that the faculty of conversation is different from the use of speech. We may have the gift of tongues
without charity, which is nothing; but conversation is that simple and
good-natured eloquence which pleases every one.

The great error of young men is to overrate their talents, as well as
to mistake the application of them. We may be assured that every appearance of conceit is correspondent with some weakness of intellect.
When a man is astonished at what he knows, it may be a proof that he
has stood on the brink of science; but it is also a proof that he has not
discovered it to be boundless and unfathomable. The ignorance of
such a person makes him loquacious and opinionative, because he has
never known what it was to be beyond his depth.

Now, the difficulty of pleasing the people we converse with consists
in not knowing what will please them; and the mistakes we make consist in this radical defect, that our principal aim in conversation is to

please ourselves. I remember, when I was a young man, I was told by a minister of the Gospel, a grave and venerable man, who had preached long, both in England and Scotland, that to please my companions and associates, I had nothing more to do than to desire and wish to do it. This is a just maxim in itself, but one which I did not then understand; for I found, that though I had the desire, I could not discover that my attempts were at all successful. Instead of that, my desire of pleasing was so ardent, that it often excited a smile at my absurdity and simplicity. Sir Walter Scott was accustomed very often to check my loquacity, and call for a song instead; and I have frequently seen him do the same with young men; for it was not age that I wanted, but experience. He had the true art of conversation. He was always amusing and instructive; and he never put any one out of countenance, but was sure to bring a modest man forward. Professor Wilson's conversation is richer and more brilliant; but then he takes sulky fits. If there be any body in the company whom he does not like, the party will not get much out of him for that night; his eyes gleam like those of a dragon; and, as a poet says of him, (Wordsworth, I think,) "he utters a short hem! at every pause; but further ventures not." The truth is, that the vivacity of youth must be tempered, the character must be established, and the means of pleasing understood, before the desire to please becomes an infallible rule in conversation. Every person soon feels disgusted with one whose whole aim is to make him laugh.

It is not the power of saying a great deal, or even of saying a great deal in the very best manner, that can make us agreeable to the hearer. It may seem paradoxical, yet it is true, that if we succeed, we must not profusely lavish the rules of the art. Though we are obliged, out of respect for female talents, to listen respectfully to Mrs. G–, Miss B–, and Mrs. S–, with mute acquiescence, they are nevertheless very tedious companions: Mrs. J–, again, is quite the reverse; I would take her as a model of a literary lady.

Whenever the desire of victory is the motive of a colloquial combatant, the charms of easy and agreeable conversation are at an end. We do not meet with our friends to fight a battle, but to be pleased and instructed. Every kind of wrangling ought to be excluded from the intercourse of friends, and the entertainer or president of a company ought to check it, at whatever expense of chagrin to the aggressors.

The best rebuke that I ever heard of this sort, or ever shall hear again, was given by the late Dr. Barclay, of Edinburgh. He was a gentleman of great suavity and mildness of disposition, and hated all kind of wrangling. So there was one day he had four other professors, five college students of the first-rate talents, and myself, to dine with him.

After the Doctor's wine began to operate a little, the young men contradicted their preceptors in almost every thing, always provoking a dispute. The seniors smiled at the young men's absurdity, and dropped the subjects. But at length two of them fastened on each other, an Englishman and an Irishman, and disputed so violently, that all social conversation was completely obstructed. It was about some point of moral philosophy, the decision of which did not signify a small pin; so their several arguments were utter nonsense. But at length, one of them, after uttering a most obstreperous sentence, came a blow on the table with his fist; on which Dr. Barclay's little terrier, that lay below it, got up, with a great bow-wow-wow! bow-wow-wow! bow-wow-wow! The Doctor gave it a gentle spurn, and, with a face of the utmost good-nature, said, "Haud your tongue, ye little stupid beast; I'm sure ye ken as little about it as ony o' them."

The reproof was successful; the gentlemen's faces both grew red, but one of them joined in the laugh till the tears ran down his cheeks. There was no more disputing that night.

There was another time, in the city of London, that I was invited to dine with a gentleman, with whom Allan Cunningham and I had several times been very happy. Before dinner, he took me aside, and said, "I have invited a Captain Selby to meet you to-night; he has been very much abroad, and his information is boundless; but he has a singular disposition to contradict every thing that is advanced by any other of the company; and then, he is so dogmatical, that he will not yield his point on any consideration. If I could get him and Mr. Walker, your friend, pitted together, we should have some fine fun, and I should give them both a rebuke which they never would forget."

Accordingly, at dinner he placed Captain Selby and Mr. Walker right over against one another, as people do two cocks which they wish to fight. At a late hour, about the time when we should have retired to coffee, the two combatants had engaged in a most desperate dispute about the antiquity of an English family, compared with that of the other disputant's own. Our first moments of enjoyment were scarcely interrupted by them, except by some looks of dissatisfaction and superiority at the trifling manner in which we were employed. At length, however, their peculiar temper broke out. Their violence bore down every attempt to change the subject, and prevented them from discovering the disconcerted looks of the company. This was the signal for the execution of Mr. H—t's project. On ringing of the bell gently and unperceived, a servant appeared to tell one of the combatants that a stranger in the next room requested to speak with him for a few minutes. The servant led him a long circular route; and in the mean time, another servant came in and asked the other disputant the same request. Consequently, they entered both at the same instant, at different doors, into the drawing-room; they bowed respectfully to one another. They both at once, however, perceived the whole force of the rebuke, and were going to sneak off at their respective doors, when the whole party broke in on them, and by their raillery and merriment made them confess both the justice and pleasantry of Mr. H–t's device. I never saw two gentlemen more obliging and complimentary to one another than these two were during the remainder of the evening.

Above all things, avoid the tricks, grimaces, and sentiments, which disgust you in others. If you find that an imperious carriage, excessive talking, sly insinuations, and the thousand methods of dragging in the subjects dearest to themselves, displease us in our acquaintances, we may believe that the same propensities in us will be disagreeable to them. And if we were not blinded by self-love, our sufferings would teach us wisdom. In this article of social intercourse there seems to be a sort of commerce, or bartering of sentiment, in which we give away what pleases us, it being understood that we receive an equal quantity of what pleases our neighbours. Generosity, too, is here inverted; for he is most amiable who, for the smallest compensation, is disposed to carry away the largest share.

You will often meet with friends who pretend to be intrusted with secrets and family affairs, and who set themselves up as a sort of general arbiters in all the concerns of their acquaintances: do not believe a word they say; it is all more from vanity, or perhaps malignity, than friendship; and always let subjects of a private nature be reserved for the ear of our friends, and never be introduced when we meet them in mixed companies; for such matters are not fitted for social and enlightened conversation.

The noblest distinction between man and the brutes is the power of forming ideas. We not only receive impressions from external objects, but we judge of the object from the impression. We treasure up our experience for future use. We combine and derive results of which all the other animals on the face of the earth are incapable. The next to this in dignity and importance, is the power of communicating our ideas. Nothing has ever appeared more wonderful to me than that, by habit, the sounds of words, which have no relation to the sense, should give me an exact picture of another man's mind, and make me acquainted with subjects of which I had never thought before. We cannot easily believe that our ideas partake of material substance: it is unnatural and absurd to say, that thin and invisible coats are perpetually flying off from the bodies which impress and act on our minds.

The images which we retain of mountains, and houses, and trees, when they are out of our sight, have as little connexion with these natural objects as our bodies have with our spirits; and yet it is true, that by a little modulation of air, and by the use of our organs in making a few sounds with letters and words, we can paint on the mind of our friend nearly the same impressions which we ourselves have received. All this is the contrivance of Infinite Wisdom, and to be accounted for with more difficulty than the immediate communication of souls, where no interruption of body intervenes to make this contrivance necessary.

Next to the perpetual wrangler, who endeavours to force truth on you by the strength of his lungs and incessant talking—next to him, I say, in the art of interrupting the pleasure of social intercourse, is the person who, by his false discernment, or affectation of purity, is sure to see something improper in almost every thing that is said, and every publication that is mentioned. This is dreadfully disgusting. I would not sit in company with a lady who mentioned the term *indelicate;* for it shows that she has been on the hunt after such expressions, and that she has treasured up for such in her mind, what was only meant for innocent pleasantries. There is no better proof of a weak understanding than to hear a man always descanting on trifles and niceties, which are really not worth speaking about. Such a man, being himself incapable of true wit and pleasantry, imagines that he contributes to the fund of general entertainment, by exposing every thing which he conceives to be false or erroneous. This is to be making rules when we should be putting them in practice, and to destroy pleasure by our disquisitions on it. Such men push themselves into company, one would think, for no other purpose than to mould the countenances of other men into the shades of dulness and formality. They attempt by their stateliness to give you a high opinion of their wisdom; and by the gravity of their features and deportment to throw a damp on all sort of freedom and hilarity. Such men produce the same effects in mixed companies as the cynic does on other men's opinions; and I have no hesitation in saying to both, that if they do not meet their friends with a disposition to be pleased, they would be wiser to stay away. What necessity do they lie under to be seeking food for their spleen where every body else is in pursuit of happiness? I do not believe that there is in human shape a character who associates with his fellow-creatures solely for the purpose of destroying their happiness. In the cases I am describing, there are other motives, which seem to proceed principally from malice. The pride of rank, or of understanding, may lurk under the grave countenance; and the vanity of displaying excellence may produce severe and contradictory remarks: but such people may be assured, that if they cannot lay aside these defects in their character, they had better never mingle in the society of their friends, for they will only render themselves more and more disagreeable.

I am sorry to make the remark, but for the sake of truth must do it, that I have generally found the ministers of the gospel most at fault in this respect. They are so accustomed to harangue others without any contradiction, that when they come into mixed societies, they cannot bear it, and too frequently grow dogmatical. I have the greatest veneration for that class of society, but must caution them against that too general failing. There are two extremes always to be carefully avoided; levity, which is too forward to please; and severity, which imposes unnecessary restraint. I have met with many almost intolerable instances of this in Scotland; and isolated country clergymen are more apt to be affected by this failing than those of a great city. In the latter, the constant friction of society has ground off all the asperities; and yet I know of some almost unbrookable instances of this character in Edinburgh, and of first-rate gentlemen too.

I found the society of London quite different; and how it should have happened with me, I know not; for I mixed freely with all sorts of respectable society; but I never met with an overweening character, either among the clergy or laity. Croly is, perhaps, a little too apt to take the lead in conversation; but then he is so exceedingly intelligent, that one is always both pleased and edified. Hood, from whom I expected a continued volley of wit, is a modest, retiring character. Reynolds more brilliant. Hook altogether inimitable, either for fun or drinking. Martin as simple in his manners as a shepherd's boy. Cruikshanks stately and solemn. But I could go over a thousand in the same way, in most of whom I was disappointed, though often most agreeably. Among the nobility and gentry I felt myself most at home, and most at my ease of all. There was no straining for superiority there. Every gentleman and lady came apparently to be pleased, and they were pleased with every thing, whether said or sung. The impression left on my mind by mingling with the first society of London, is that of perfection, and what I would just wish society to be.

But this is all extraneous matter–I must return to general principles; and it being quite evident that every man is not fitted for conducting conversation, yet I aver, that it is our own faults if we are not able to enjoy it. It is to this point, if our object be to please ourselves and associates, that we should direct our attention. The display of superior talents excites envy. You never see professional men succeed in conversation, unless they possess great modesty in speaking of their own profession. And even those who have a pleasant flow of genuine humour, will not find channels for it in every company; but every man or woman may possess, if they choose, the power and capacity of being pleased, and this will fit them for all kinds of innocent conversation. We must have the power of attending, as well as of speaking; and the former is of infinitely more importance than the latter; because by speaking, suppose in the very best manner, we discover the extent of our understanding, and sometimes of our vanity; but by hearing as we ought to do, we discover our cheerfulness and humility, without the imputation of assumption or vanity.

It is a fact, however it may be received, that the fair sex excel more in conversation than ours. I do not intend to flatter the women, for I have flattered them too much already, nor will I pretend to say that they speak less; but the beauty of their conversation is, that they listen to and hear a great deal more. They have some way an acuteness of perception, which enables them to follow the most rapid discourse, and a superiority of candour which prevents them from misrepresenting it. They never wrangle from slowness of apprehension, nor for the purpose of misleading or perplexing their hearers; and, therefore, all men of superior minds have preferred the conversation of the fair sex to that of their own. Were they to add a competent knowledge of all proper colloquial subjects, they would enchant mankind still more; and, God knows, their power over us is sufficient already!

But, for all their faults, we must confess that nature has fitted women for conversation in a superior degree to our own sex. Their minds are more refined and delicate than ours, their imaginations more vivid, and their expressions more at command. When sweetness and modesty are joined to intelligence, the charms of their conversation are irresistible. I, therefore, earnestly wish and pray that the ladies, who have so much power over the whole progress of society, and can model mankind as they please, would take the pains to model some plan of rational solidity. I assure them, I am in earnest. At present they justly and properly take the lead in all conversations, and are uniformly listened to with respect, and the reverence with which we approach them is rather incompatible with that playfulness which we are obliged to assume to humour them, by conforming to their manner, of which we are incapable.

I must always regard the society of London as the pink of what I have seen in the world. I met with most of the literary ladies, and confess that I liked them better than the blue-stockings of Edinburgh. Their general information is not superior to that of their northern sisters, perhaps it may be said that it is less determined; but, then, they never assume so much. The society of London that I mixed with is, as I have said before, just such a model as I would always desire to see. There was no wrangling; none whatever; not even on political creeds. They intermixed all in the most perfect harmony; and if such a thing as the different sides chanced to be mentioned, it was by way of joke. Mr. Holmes was, however, a very arbitrary gentleman among them, but a fellow of infinite good-humour.

But to return to the power of women in general, which, in society highly polished, may be said to be omnipotent, therefore they must take the lead in reforming it. There are just two things to be attained, which will sufficiently qualify them for this arduous task of improving mankind. First, they must improve themselves, and then must studiously honour and distinguish men of learning, virtue, and genius. The first would make the fops acquire some sort of learning in their own defence; and the second would make them ashamed of themselves, if such a thing were possible.

The ladies have, moreover, the advantage of going wherever their fancy leads them, with little danger of being envied or affronted. A man of learning is responsible for his opinions, and is generally as positive as he is learned. But the fair sex have the power of dressing science in her gayest robes, of laughing us into wisdom, and conquering us when seeming to yield. It is, indeed, but a little way that the most enlightened of the human race can descend into the mysteries of nature and providence which surround them; yet, if we do not render ourselves incapable by our carelessness, a certain degree of knowledge on all subjects is nearly competent to all. There are, then, common grounds on which, as rational creatures, we daily meet. How useful and how improving might our conversation be rendered! We might discuss, in the first place, the topics on which every man's senses give him sufficient information.

I have been often amused at the general topics of conversation discussed by men respectable in life. The quarter from which the wind blows, and how long it has travelled on the same current, and the effects it has on the flocks, fields, and cattle, is a grand and never-ending subject, though all know it alike well. Then the different dishes and wines are to be discussed, and, above all things, the sauces. O, it is amazing what grand discoveries have been made in these! I once heard a reverend professor assert, that he had of late made a very important discovery. What was it, think you? That beet radish made a pickle greatly superior to the radishes or cabbage of Savoy!

This, to be sure, is all very trivial; but it is harmless, and may lead to deeper researches into the arcana of nature. It is, at all events, better than circulating slander and insinuations tending to mischief. The illiberal prejudices and ridiculous customs of the world, compel me to descant on such trifles, as they occur in all parties where business is not conducted, and where friendship dare not unbosom itself. But, alas! what a pity that reasonable creatures should eat and drink together to so little purpose! It is one of the unaccountable characters of our nature, that in those companies where trifles form the principal topics of conversation, no man or woman will venture a wise or deep remark. We choose rather to appear what we are not, than fail in what we wish to be. But surely in all such parties the finer and more aërial portion of our constitution, the soul, ought to be gratified as well as the palate.

As I am obliged to draw my pictures from my own circumscribed observation, I am compelled reluctantly to confess, that I have often heard the ladies complain of the frivolity of our conversation; and that where they expected the finest wheat, they found only chaff. They would be wiser to hold their tongues on this matter, as they themselves are often the cause of that frivolity; and they little know what is said of them in certain situations. It is a pity there should be any reason of complaint on either side; for it is not because good sense is banished from among us, but because the two sexes are absurdly pleased mutually to converse together under a mask, until the whole becomes a scene of impertinence and folly, where the great contest seems to be, who shall best conceal their ignorance, and not display their knowledge. Hence vivacity is often substituted for wit, and pleasing trifles dressed out in the gaudiest colours; and thus our intercourse with the world may amuse us for a while, but can yield us no solid or lasting advantage. Let the fair sex, then, be the first to pull off the mask themselves, and they will soon prevail on their acquaintances of the other sex to unmask also. It is their bounden duty to set the example; for we are much more afraid of them than they are of us, and much more influenced by their manners than they are by ours. If once their general conduct be moulded into the form of advice, it is irresistible. How lovely to see modesty mixed with learning, wit with good-nature, and a taste in dress with a taste for something of more intense value.

But if you find, that among your associates the disease is so inveterate as not to be cured by the example of the fair, the wise, and the good; if folly shall continue to be predominant, clamour to overtop reason, and scandal triumph over decency; then it is time to do as I have done; to retire from the world, and in some obscure retreat, with as many friends as choose to follow you, try to seek wisdom in the shade, disencumbered of scoffers and evil-speakers; for truly *a whole-*

some tongue is a tree of life; but perverseness therein is a breach of the spirit.

From my choice of the above text, it is manifest that I wish seriously all scandal to be banished from well-bred society. People of the higher walks of life, if ignorant, which they sometimes are, seem to be most addicted to scandal. You would scarcely believe that the little tricks and failings of the peasantry are often minutely detailed at a great man's table. There is an elevation in rank which must be supported, either by dignity of character or by a comparison with the vulgar. There lies the fountain-head of their malevolent talk. But it is only an invidious rising on other men's defects; a vain attempt to scramble over a wall of mud, in which you do no more than shew your ambition and foul your clothes.

Let me entreat, then, of every Christian and genteel community to check every attempt at the introduction of that vile ingredient into social conversation. What pleasure can it give to any rational being to hear that a man who is not present to defend himself, is suspected of a very wicked or ridiculous action? Is it not most unfair to tell a story to a dozen of people, which cannot be told to the person most deeply interested? And why does one expose himself to the danger of circulating a lie? When a man or woman brandishes this weapon of mischief among their friends, it is a clear proof that they are unfit for the rational enjoyment of their company. There may be some present who will give full credit to the account, though, perhaps, the retailer may be the twentieth person from the original. This is stabbing a man behind his back; and for his own character's sake, no one should introduce topics of scandal and detraction. The heart that believes them is malicious, and the vanity that indulges in them is contemptible. Keep, therefore, the apothegm of the wise man always before your eyes and uppermost in your heart. *A wholesome tongue is a tree of life; but perverseness therein is a breach of the spirit.*

I have just one other observation to make before leaving this subject, and I am afraid it may be thought by many to come but ill from the pen of one who has concocted so many manifest, though amusing falsehoods. It is religious conversation, of which I have as yet said nothing. Now, I never like to hear religion brought into a large company as matter of general conversation. It is a dangerous topic, and apt to be productive of more evil than good, there being so many scoffers and Deists in almost every community; and I have even heard some of the wildest blasphemy poured unblushingly and triumphantly forth. Therefore I would not have the mild and humble religion of Jesus even risked against such a battery. But, among friends, whose hearts and sentiments are known to each other, what can be so sweet or so advantageous as occasional conversation on the principles of our mutual belief, and the doctrines of grace and salvation? Suffer me, then, to detail a few of the advantages which, by the blessing of God, we are likely to enjoy by indulging in this blissful communication of sentiments, and abstracting ourselves from worldly concerns.

One great advantage, then, which the fearers of God derive from conferring together, is growth and improvement in the spiritual life. The words we hear in conversation, especially from those we love, have a surprising influence on the turn of the mind, the feelings of the heart, and our behaviour in life. I have seen many instances, and I relate it with pleasure, that a simple hint hath raised and cherished devout affections, hath caught hold of a man when he was tottering on the verge of some foul transaction, and been the means of re-establishing him in virtue, and in a laudable course of action every way becoming a sincere Christian. I have known even a conversation held in a dream have a powerful effect on the heart in warning one from approaching evil. And I know that many a man hath felt the emotions of gratitude stir in his breast by being casually put in mind of God's great loving-kindness towards him. A single expression from those we esteem concerning the excellency of our religion, and the surpassing love of Jesus for fallen and ruined mankind, or concerning the dignity, the reality, and the beauty of virtue, amidst all the corruption, confusion, and dissipation, which like a cloud of wrath hath overspread the world,—such a genial hint, I say, will seldom fall in vain. It awakens in the soul admiration and love to God; it kindles a warm desire in the hearer towards virtue and holiness, cherishing the same desire in the heart of the speaker. How often, too, hath soft persuasion pacified wrath and stemmed the impetuous tide of passion! How often hath it excited pity and commiseration, and allayed the boisterous intentions of revenge and cruelty, controlled a friend's criminal desires, made him alter his purpose, and preserve his innocence! How beautiful and forcible, then, are these words of the great King of Israel! They ought to be engraved on the tablet of every heart. *A wholesome tongue is a tree of life; but perverseness therein is a breach of the spirit.*

I could quote many passages of holy writ to the same purport, not one of which is to be despised or neglected; such as, "A word fitly spoken, is like apples of gold in pictures of silver." "The words of the wise are as goads, and as nails fastened in sure places by the masters of the assemblies." "Let, therefore, no corrupt communication proceed out of your mouth; but that which is good to the use of edifying." "Be ye filled with the spirit, speaking among yourselves mutually." "Let the word of Christ dwell in you richly in all wisdom, teaching and admonishing one another." All these are maxims bearing the same stamp, and from the very highest source.

Let us, then, endeavour to dispose ourselves to an exercise so salutary. We can never be at a loss for materials, having the whole Scriptures of truth before us. We may converse on the failings and virtues of the patriarchs of old, and how the judgments and mercies of God were exercised toward them and their families. We may trace the history of the most wonderful people that ever inhabited the face of the globe, the prophecies concerning them, and their extraordinary fulfilment. All the prophecies concerning our Saviour, from the day that man first fell in Paradise, to that in which the Son of the Highest came in the likeness of sinful flesh to save us. Such communications can hardly fail to warm our hearts with the love of God, love to one another, give us the command of our passions, and bend us to the practice of righteousness. We might farther enlarge on the nature and beauty of every Christian virtue, the obligations to the practice of it derived from the light of nature, and strengthened by revelation of the love and gospel of Jesus. Indulge, then, in this heavenly conversation, and you shall ever bless the day that made you acquainted with such friends; for in very deed *a wholesome tongue is a tree of life; but perverseness therein is a breach in the spirit.*

Sermon IV

Soldiers

"From whence come wars and fighting among you? Sirs, ye are
brethren; why do ye harm one to another?"

IN the holy Scriptures, innumerable reasons are suggested to prevail
on men to repress every angry passion, to persuade them to do justly,
to love mercy, walk humbly, cultivate the kind affections, and cherish
the spirit of benevolence. But though we were at first made upright,
we have sought out many inventions, and, alas! how many of these
have been evil ones! All men are formed and upheld by the same
common Father; therefore they are brethren; for he hath formed of
one blood all the kindreds of the earth. *Ye are all, then, brethren; why do ye
harm one to another?* If princes, before they commit any atrocious act of
public injustice; if lawgivers, before they rashly enact any law leading
to oppression, slavery, and blood, would but take time to consider,
pause, and think, before they pass the Rubicon; just recollect simply
that all men are their brethren, and that they are accountable creatures,—what carnage, what misery of the human race might often be
saved!

But princes and great men, who are the means of stirring up wars
and commotions among their fellow-men, generally live in luxury in
their palaces, far from the battle's alarm, and are but little sensible of
the miseries that accompany the wars which they themselves have
raised: even the people in common life are not, I am certain, apprised
half enough of the horrors which accompany it; for as soon as we are
able to attend to any thing, we hear and read about war and all the
barbarous acts of destruction, until we become not only familiar with
them, but delighted, valuing the hero still the more in proportion to
the thousands he has destroyed. We never stop to consider how horri-
ble these scenes are, because what we know of them we generally
learn at an age when the mind receives ideas implicitly, admires every
thing that appears great, and never loses those early impressions, which
remain indelibly fixed in it for ever. Hence it is, that if a person in low
life, to gratify his avarice or revenge, waylays and murders another,
we shudder at such cruelty; but if a statesman, to gratify his pride, his

ambition, or aspiration at fame or dominion, forms a plan, in the execution of which a million of innocent unoffending people shall by the sword be hurried into eternity, we applaud his valour and the daring greatness of his spirit. What is the fortune of the two culprits? The one is dragged to the gallows as he deserves; but the greater culprit of the two, the infinitely more criminal, is lauded by gaping crowds of slavish and stupid people, and perhaps gets himself possessed of half the riches of a kingdom.

I myself know nothing of the art of war; but have often turned my attention to the pride and ambition which occasion it, and to the destruction which it spreads among the human race; and I would fain lay before those who recklessly begin wars and conduct them, a few things which deserve their serious consideration.

Consider the small accession of comfort or delight that springs from opulence or large possessions. The vanity of ambition and all worldly grandeur—the injustice of all private fightings and public wars. But, most of all, consider that we have the clearest prospects of a life to come; and in what manner, say twenty thousand souls of neighbouring nations, ascending together from the carnage of a battle-field, will think and talk of the ridiculous scene which they have just quitted; and how they have (for they know not what) thus hurried themselves from all the kindred ties of life into the presence of their judge, with all their imperfections on their heads.

There is another thing, which it is strange kings and conquerors have never considered, which is, that whatever they may lose, they never gain any thing by war, even though their troops have been rather successful. Look at all the wars of Europe for hundreds of years, and you will see, that, after millions of human beings had been sacrificed, at the end all things were settled the same as when the war began, and the same boundaries remained to be peopled anew. It is really so ridiculous, that one can hardly think on it as the doings of rational creatures and Christians.

After the campaigns of Buonaparte, and the slaughter of so many millions among the most civilised nations on the face of the earth, and which ended so completely in smoke, I really thought there would never be any more wars in Europe, but that all would be settled by arbitration; and I have still a hope that, in this enlightened age, the days of battle and war are far hence.

It would appear from history, that the rulers of kingdoms have often kindled up the flames of war, they scarcely knew why or wherefore; so that upon a retrospective view, historians and politicians have been quite at a loss how to account for it. The history of every war is very like a scene I once saw in Nithsdale. Two boys from different schools met one fine day upon the ice. They eyed each other with rather jealous and indignant looks, and with defiance on each brow.

"What are ye glowrin' at, Billy?"

"What's that to you? I'll look where I have a mind, an' hinder me if ye daur."

A hearty blow was the return to this, and there such a battle began. It being Saturday, all the boys of both schools were on the ice; and the fight instantly became general and desperate. At one time they fought with missile weapons, such as stones and snow-balls; but at length they coped in a rage, and many bloody raps were liberally given and received. I went up to try if I could pacify them; for by this time a number of little girls had joined the affray, and I was afraid they would be killed; so, addressing the one party, I asked what they were pelting the others for? What they had done to them?

"O, naething at a', man; we just want to gie them a good thrashin'."

After fighting till they were quite exhausted, one of the principal heroes stepped forth between, covered with blood, and his clothes to tatters, and addressed the belligerent parties thus:

"Weel; I'll tell you what we'll do wi' ye: if ye'll let us alane, we'll let you alane." There was no more of it; the war was at an end, and the boys scattered away to their play. I thought at the time, and have often thought since, that that trivial affray was the best epitome of war in general, that I had ever seen. Kings and ministers of state are just a set of grown-up children, exactly like the children I speak of, with only this material difference, that instead of fighting out the needless quarrels they have raised, they sit in safety and look on, hound out their innocent but servile subjects to battle, and then, after a waste of blood and treasure, are glad to make the boy's conditions, "If ye'll let us alane, we'll let you alane."

It would be much more conformable to what nature dictates, for kings or their ministers to fight it out in person, or each by a champion, like the Israelites and Philistines. But who among them ever testifies the noble feeling and sentiments of King David, when, for a particular offence of his, a great plague was to come on his subjects, who were innocent? who can cease to admire the generosity and disinterestedness of the great Psalmist of Israel at that trying juncture? "And David spake unto the Lord and said, Lo! I have sinned, and I have done wickedly; but as for these sheep, what have they done? let thine hand, I pray thee, be against me and my father's house."

But wars have been since the beginning of the world, and cannot always be avoided; but there are some rules which I think never should be violated,—for even that nation, which by its injustice hath excited against itself a just war, has rights which it would be the highest injustice to invade. Whatever is repulsive to nature and reason, I take to be unlawful in war. Nothing should be done that tends merely to exasperate and make the breach wider, and lengthen out the contest—nothing but what hath a tendency to bring the war to a close. Incursions into the interior parts of an enemy's country, to burn their villages, drive their cattle, robbing and killing the defenceless peasantry, is unjust and cruel in the extreme. These had no hand in raising the war—they never gave your government or yourselves any offence, nor had it in their power to do so; why then wreak your vengeance on them? The fortune of war is apt to change, and a cutting remembrance of such needless and unavailing acts of barbarity may provoke a dreadful retaliation. It is, moreover, a paltry, pilfering way of making war dishonourable to yourselves and the country to whom you belong.

There are a few more general rules which you, as Christian soldiers, should never break through. An ambassador, a mediator, or hostage, are never to be injured in their persons or property—soldiers never cut down or fired upon after they have laid down their arms and asked quarter—the wounded are not to be slaughtered on the field, nor prisoners killed or barbarously used—the sword never to be drawn against old men, children, or women, and the persons of the latter to be held as sacred. These are a few of the rules and restrictions which ought to be observed among all civilised and especially Christian armies. They are often violated; but, brave soldiers, remember this, that whenever you do violate any of them, you injure your characters as men, as well as that of your commander, and the country that gave you your birth and education.

But, after every deduction which the most unbounded charity can make for the vices of mankind, I am afraid we must allow, that there is some malignity in the heart, before we can perceive the glory of warlike achievements acquired over the bodies of the wounded and the dead. I declare to you, soldiers, that I shudder every time I think of the scene that a field of battle presents; and I am persuaded, that though I had the strength and the courage of Hector, yet I could never have brought them to the test. What a strange, unnatural thing is a general war! If men were allowed to go on increasing their numbers and possessions, this world would be a tolerable residence for such a length of time as we are intended by Providence to continue in it. We should, indeed, still be exposed to the diseases and pains which are incident to our imperfect state. But, as if these were not sufficient to employ the rancour of one part of mankind, and to exercise the patience of another, or as if the world were not wide enough, we must contend tribe against tribe, and nation against nation, until a certain number, as many as can be wanted, are killed, and then the remainder are glad to make peace on the boy of Thornhill's terms.

War is, without doubt, a great evil; and has originated in the evil and malevolent passions of our nature, which seem to form a primitive part of our constitution, and which neither the reasonings of the philosopher, nor the injunctions of religion, have been able to eradicate; but self-preservation is its only legitimate object; and where this can be obtained by other means, recourse cannot justifiably be had to war. In this clear principle all writers on ethics are agreed; and it is by a reference to this principle alone, that every war must be ultimately vindicated or condemned. Were governments scrupulous in their adherence to those great principles of universal equity which are common to states and individuals, and by which the rights of both ought to be adjusted, wars would cease to desolate and depopulate the earth. The very existence of war, indeed, implies the absence of law. It is an attempt to supply its place by a recurrence to those first principles of our nature which prompt us instinctively to self-defence. The war of nations rests precisely on the same grounds for its justification as that of individuals. When men congregate together, it becomes necessary to unite their force to accomplish objects to which individual exertion would be inadequate; but there is no theological difference between public and private wars; they rest on the same ground, and must be justified or condemned by a reference to the same principles.

It has been maintained by many divines that all wars are unlawful; and that a Christian cannot, under any circumstances, be justified in destroying his fellow-creatures. Yet, though I entertain a detestation for all wars, public or private, I must be allowed to question the soundness of this doctrine. That the Scriptures uniformly describe wars in their proper characters, as crimes and judgments, is literally true, and their origin is ascribed to our lawless and malignant passions, as in the first clause of our text. But the profession of a soldier is no where forbidden in Scripture, that I remember of. On the contrary, when the soldiers came to John the Baptist, and asked him what it was their duty to do, he answered them, "Do violence to no man, neither accuse any falsely, and be content with your wages." This last is a hint the same as I gave before, that they were not to plunder or pilfer; but there is nothing in the injunction of the prophet desiring them to relinquish their profession. That a soldier may be a good man and a sincere Christian I am well aware, both from history and personal knowledge; but I have a higher authority than either. Consider what our

Saviour says of a soldier and officer, "I have not found so great faith, no not in Israel."

But the application of the principles of morality to individual cases of war is very difficult. The reference of self-preservation is in many instances too abstract and remote for the direction of private consciences; but it is essential to the general interests of belligerent nations, that their modes of action in warfare as well as peace should be regulated by some constant and known rule. This is admitted by the existence of that artificial jurisprudence, entitled "the law of nations." Now, though this code has grown insensibly into usage, without any form, acknowledgment, or known original, yet this is the very law which I would advise every soldier of honour not to invalidate. I have enumerated all such already as strike my inexperience as essential, and I repeat the remark merely to bring in one very singular custom which seems to be universally admitted as the law of nations.

It is that which relates to newly discovered countries, the sovereignty of which belongs to the prince or state by whose subjects it was first discovered. Now, nothing can be more fanciful, or less supported by any considerations of reason, than this, that the transient occupation and idle ceremonies which accompany it should confer the sovereignty of that country upon any one. No stipulation can be produced by which the rest of the world have bound themselves to the admission of such a pretension. Yet not admitted, it would necessarily lead to endless bloody wars and contentions. It is thus that utility makes laws for itself. The rule above stated possesses the great requisites of determination and certainty, and has long been generally, though silently, acquiesced in, from the manifest certainty that no power has the influence or ability to procure the adoption of a better rule. But I must now return to a few of the moral definitions of war.

In the rudest state of society the savage is found in friendship with his own tribe, and at war with his neighbours. The country, to a certain extent, has been from the beginning of the world in possession of the ancestors of this great and illustrious tribe, which every one of them are, and every one the greatest and the most ancient. The sun was created to shine upon them. The Great Spirit had been exceedingly bountiful to them. The hills, the rivulets, the woods, and the wild beasts, all belonged to them alone; and if a stranger dared to trespass on those ancient and sacred rights, he was sure to suffer for his rashness. Then the yell of war resounded through both savage communities, and an exterminating war begun. We cannot read without shudderings of horror, the dreadful resentment which burned in the bosoms of these unenlightened heathens. We follow the captives of the victorious to the cruel, savage scene which precedes their destruction, and rejoice in those liberal arts and the mild spirit of Christianity which have taught us humanity.

Though it is to be hoped that wars and wickedness will cease throughout the world, yet, on a retrospect, there seems often to have been a moral necessity for them to purge a land of enormous wickedness. Of all the sanguinary nations who ever inhabited the face of the globe, there were never any like the chosen people of God, the Turks and Tartars not excepted; and yet their most ruthless murders of men, women, and children, seem to have been done mostly by God's express commands. What shall we say then? The Creator and Governor of the universe cannot do wrong; and, as sure as his word is truth, hath he ordered the total extinction of nations and families. Therefore, it is only by the spread of Christianity over the world, and the cultivation of universal love and peace, that the halcyon days predicted by the prophet can ever be accomplished. "The wolf shall dwell with the lamb, and the leopard shall lie down with the kid; and the calf and the young lion and the fatling together, and a little child shall lead them; and the cow and the bear shall feed, their young ones shall lie down together; and the lion shall eat straw like the ox. The sucking child shall play on the hole of the asp, and the weaned child shall put his hand on the cockatrice's den. For the earth shall be full of the knowledge of the Lord, as the waters cover the sea."

Christianity has yearly and daily more and more influence over our conduct; and we enjoy a wider range of pleasures—innocent, agreeable, and fraught with intellectual improvement—than our fathers did; yet we are no less destructive in fields of battle than they were, but have rather improved in our modes of general destruction. In this state of human affairs, then, there is nothing left but to invite all men of wit and learning, all who are possessed of humanity, and all who are interested in the peace and happiness of the world, to unite their endeavours and talents to bring the system of destruction into discredit, that the sword may not devour for ever. Why should ambitious men appeal either to the present age or posterity for the glory of their character? Let us never be dazzled with what is splendid, unless it be also just. The endeavours of the learned and wise alone, united in the support of humanity, would be more than sufficient to bear down the clamorous desires of ambition, and quiet the turbulence of mankind; and to this glorious combination every true minister of the gospel of Jesus is bound to contribute a part.

I know that the soldier will reply to this, that it is an ideal triumph of humanity over reason, for that war is a disease which never can be cured, because in most instances there is no safety except in carrying it on. There is no tribunal to which he can appeal from an armed force; and nothing can resist its operation save force opposed to force, and violence to violence. It is too true; the study of the art of war, however, is the most dangerous of any. It leads to no aim or end besides the taking of life. The lion roars for his prey, yet when he is satiated he returns to his den; but the thirst of military fame is never quenched. Every victory is a new starting place from which to unleash the dogs of havoc and of war. I am sensible that mine are only the feeble attempts of a compassionate heart, to heal the wounds which have never ceased to bleed since the second man in the world committed the first murder; but if they should be instrumental in saving the honour of one individual of my countrymen, or the life of one fellow-creature, though I may not be alive to enjoy it, I shall not lose my reward. Let me conclude this rambling discourse by a quotation, which I have always deemed powerful, from one of our ancient dramatists—whom I do not know.

> "The dreadful harass of the war is o'er,
> And Slaughter, that, from yestermorn till even,
> With giant steps passed striding o'er the field,
> Besmeared and horrid with the blood of nations;
> Now weary sits among the mangled heaps,
> And slumbers o'er her prey."

Sermon V

To Young Men

"My son, if sinners entice thee, consent thou not."

THERE was never any precept given from the tongue or pen of man more cogent than this; for in the choice of our friends and connexions principally consists the virtue or the guilt, the happiness or misery, of every man through life. Taking this as a position which admits of no contradiction, I shall proceed to point out some rules whereby to choose our early friends.

I have been always happy in the choice of my intimate friends, excepting, perhaps, in one instance; and I shall, therefore, give my young friends such directions in the choice of theirs as reason and my slight experience shall direct.

I remember when I first entered into genteel society, which was not till after the year 1813, I thought it the easiest matter possible to gain the affections of every person, of whatever age, and to live in habits of intimacy and friendship with them. Alas! how soon I found myself mistaken; for, to my astonishment, the very men with whom I had been so happy over night, who had crammed me with flattery more than I could hold—and it is a dish with which I am not very apt to be satiated—who had invited me to their houses, not on one day but every day that suited my convenience, would the next day, when I addressed them in the kindest and most affectionate way I was able, stare me in the face, and shrink from the gloveless hand of the poor poet, without uttering a word! "Go thy ways, Paul," said I to myself; "when I have a convenient season I will speak to thee on this matter."

But this reflection relates only to my own sex. If I have ever had reason to complain of the other, it has been on the contrary side. Blessings on them! for their kindnesses have often put me out of countenance so that never a word I could say. In the choice of these for friends and partners, I shall have something to say by-and-by. In the mean time, I shall lay a few injunctions on such young men as I respect and love; and, as I have a heart, I do not know a living soul whom I do not wish well.

Youth is desirous of enjoyment, but free from that selfishness which we acquire by experience in the world. The education of all young men of a certain rank of life, whatever may be their future destination, is conducted on nearly the same plan, imposes nearly the same restraints, and their times of relaxation from the fatigues of study and application are spent in nearly the same pursuits and arrangements. The consequence is, that, till a young man is sent to the academy, every boy he meets with at his father's house, low and high, rich or poor, is an intimate and bosom friend, even though he should have known him only for a few days. They will cry at parting, and forget one another in shorter time than they have been together. This is the first opening of a flower, which will shed its fragrance over our whole life, if we cherish and cultivate it. I am far from blaming those first emanations of the human heart, and I think no system of education can be perfect by which they are not encouraged. It very frequently happens, that lasting friendships spring from the transient intercourse of children; but the pursuits, habits, and professions of men, are so different from the links which connected them in early life, that this cannot always take place. It is generally, therefore, at a more advanced period that we form those attachments which continue to old age, and which end only with our lives. The time for doing this, is when we are entering on the business of life, and preparing for the stations which we intend to occupy. In other words, a young friend of mine is just pushing his vessel from the shore, and it can certainly do him no harm to consider a little who will make the best companions of his voyage. Then is the time to keep in mind the warning voice, "*If sinners entice thee, consent thou not.*"

You might account me a selfish old man, and tainted with the disease of worldly prudence, were I to continue the metaphor, and maintain that you should allow none to accompany you in the hazardous voyage except such as you could employ at the helm or the sails; or that you should choose your friends as you choose your clothes—to set you off to advantage and keep you warm. But this is not the advice I give you, for it is contrary to my own feelings and experience. Friendship purely disinterested, is that only which deserves the name. In the common intercourse of mankind, indeed, we call every man our friend who is not our enemy; and he, too, sometimes, by way of derision. But if a man speak well of us in our absence, or take a little trouble in promoting our interests, he is immediately styled our friend, and certainly with some propriety. But a cynic might say, that surely selfishness is the universal character among mankind, since trivial acts of kindness are so much noted. In this commerce of courtesy and affection, no man is deceived; and we may generally consider it more as an excess of politeness than an error of the heart. But there is still much benevolence in the world, and as I am speaking to young men, I hope I shall be trusted when I say, that they must have particular friends as well as general ones; and the characters of the former of these I shall endeavour to point out.

Be sure, then, to mix prudence with the first dictates of the heart in such a choice. Seek not for your associates and bosom friends in the wilds of romance, but in the world—in the labyrinth of life—among people subject to the same vicissitudes as yourself. Rash friendships are never lasting; and if you think every person you meet with of open and frank character, whom you like for some congeniality of disposition with yourself, and desire to knit him to you for ever, it is almost ten to one that you will find yourself disappointed. Some little unexpected jealousies will occasionally happen between people who truly love one another, the rude shock of which would easily overset a hasty and precarious friendship; you will therefore do better to cultivate the dispositions of mind which will in due time secure you valuable and lasting friendships, founded on virtue and similarity of dispositions, which will ultimately prove of more value than making to yourselves friends at once.

I know some young people who choose their friends by the eye—the same as they choose a coat or vest. I do not disapprove of this altogether; for, there certainly is something in every human countenance less or more attractive, or less or more repulsive; and I would trust more to Lavater than to Spurzheim. But never once form the least estimate of a character until you hear him or her speak. The tones of the voice are the best symptoms in the world whereby to form a true and immediate judgment of a character. They are the chords of the soul; and if you have any ear for music, you may as easily judge of the sterling value of the character as of a violin or an organ. There is not a single feature of a character which is not delineated in the tones of the voice. I have been often taken with the appearance and countenances of young men in public assemblies, and yet the very first time I heard them speak, I found at once that they were consummate blockheads. But whenever I found the countenance and the voice accord in sweetness, I could then form an estimate of the character, which, in all my life, I have never had occasion to change. But there is one thing, I think, I may affirm—that in the whole world, among human beings as among sheep, there is not one character, countenance, nor voice, exactly like another; and yet, among all this diversity, you will scarcely find two individuals in whom there is not some point of contrast which may render them agreeable and acceptable to each other. We are, indeed, strangely and wonderfully made.

But it is vain to expect that from such slight approximations of character a lasting union can be established. Many young men of shallow minds, however, are deceived by such incidental instances of similarity, and expect that they have found a steady and sincere friend, because, perchance, they were pleased with him in one of his moods. I am far from inculcating a jealous or suspicious temper in your intercourse with the world, for this is a character I abhor, even when I find it under grey hairs; and I do so because I can never be sure whether the owner has acquired it by reflection on his own character or the villany of the world.

But when this is the temper of a young man, there is no ambiguity in the case; because, he has had no experience to suggest its necessity, and you may almost depend on it that extreme caution and jealousy in youth will turn out villany in old age. "Let no such man be trusted."

You ought, however, to be prudent in the choice of your friends; not because you suspect their integrity, or because you are afraid of being deceived, but because, on full trial, they may be deficient in that congeniality of mind which is the true cement of friendship, and which unites the heart of one man to another. This sort of prudence I think fair and honourable; nor is it any impeachment of your acquaintance that they have not all the qualities which your heart desires. But remember this, if ever your adopted friend should endeavour to persuade you into a house or company which is improper, thenceforth drop all intimacy with him, and remember this sterling adage, "*My son, if sinners entice thee, consent thou not.*"

Where there is not virtue, there can be no real friendship. There may be associations of knaves, and their common interests may give them laws and bind them for some time together; but you may be assured that any friendship which deserves the name must be free from all suspicion, and built on the integrity of your friend's character, and the purity of your own. There are blemishes in all characters; certain little defects arising from constitution or temper, which we should all be better without, but which we are not able to relinquish. Therefore, if we expect absolute perfection, we must look for men in other worlds, to whom we may unbosom ourselves. We have, besides, no right to demand this perfection, as we must all be conscious how many imperfections we have ourselves. Therefore, those blemishes never ought to prevent, or interrupt, friendship. The law of kindness on this head is to think on our own blemishes when we observe and pity those of our friends; and if they have good qualities which we find endear them to us, we must forgive their failings, and patiently endure what we are not able to prevent. But it is of use for us to know, that the man is best qualified for friendship who has benevolent affections to cover his faults. I would have you always choose that person for your friend whose spots are best visible when he is with those whom he loves; but, when I write to you on this subject, I request you to remark the wide difference between those unavoidable blemishes which are found in the characters of worthy men, and the vices which are found only in the haunts of wickedness. You see a good man striving against his weakness, and after gaining strength daily, finally to overcome it; but it is the nature of vice to debase the character; and every act of wickedness, whatever it is, makes you worse than you were before. You become gradually to have less and less power to resist temptation, and are less afraid of the discovery of your guilt. Never think of choosing a friend unless you can live with him by day or by night without seeing the example of vicious conduct: and never associate cordially with men whose example or advice appears to lead you from the path of truth and uprightness; for there is a way that leadeth unto life, and another that as certainly leadeth to destruction; therefore, "*O my son, if sinners entice thee, consent thou not.*"

It is a fact hardly reconcilable with reason, but it is nevertheless true, that the path of destruction is always most irrecoverably dangerous when we are found in it with those we love. Their persuasive voice and animating example conceal from us the pit and the snare that lie before us. I have known more young men ruined in their prospects by improper attachments than by all other casualties put together; therefore, I intreat you, to keep company and converse with those alone who will do you honour by their virtues, and instruct you by their example.

It is the common practice among vicious young men to debauch the sober; and they seem to enjoy a sort of malignant pleasure when they succeed. Such companions never discover to you at once the whole deformity of their character. Their own gradual defection from what they once were, has taught them the most successful methods of infusing the poison of vice, and yet concealing its odiousness. I suppose Satan himself would have been less dangerous to mankind if he had never been an angel of light. Men of this character, from what motive I know not, whether it be to have access to their purse, to have companions in sin, or for the love of evil for its own sake, seem to consider sober and virtuous young men as fair game, whom, by every means in their power, they are to hunt into their toils. It therefore becomes my duty to warn you of your danger, and I do it with a thousand times less anxiety than I should try to reclaim you if fairly gone astray.

There is an inherent modesty in the innocence of youth, which rejects vice. This is a guard which the providence of God has placed over us, when we are in the most unsuspecting and unprotected condition. In leading you astray, therefore, the artful will not discover to you for a long time the whole length they mean to carry you. They will even counterfeit virtue and disinterestedness, till they get you entangled in the net which they have spread; they will lay hold of your affections to corrupt your heart. But while I am setting before you the character of a kind of men who make it their employment to deceive unadvised youth, I am far from wishing you to believe that your acquaintance in general design to mislead you. On the contrary, if you begin life with too much caution, and with great fear of being deceived, you will disgust those who are worthy of your friendship, and lay yourself more open to the attacks of the artful and designing. You need not, therefore, hang out a flag of defiance to tempt them to try the powers of their ingenuity on your prudence. It is the wicked only who fleeth when no man pursueth. Simple integrity is a better defence to a young man's virtue than excessive caution and pretended superior prudence.

But there is a prudence in your own heart, which you must exercise in the choice of your friends, as well as rejecting the unworthy. You must judge of the character of your associates by the effect produced in your own mind; and if the same person who engages your affection promotes your knowledge and your virtue, why should you not cherish him in your heart as a dear and confidential friend? If a man can retire from the company of the wicked when he discovers their character, and feels himself injured by it, he is as perfectly safe as if he were always suspecting danger. It is to this point I request you to direct your attention in the choice of your friends. There are persons of generous dispositions, and of easy and frank manners, who are in all respects worthy of your confidence, if they have no views which may be the more dangerous to you as you love them for their good qualities. Vice is sanctioned to the mind of a young man when it appears only as some spot or blemish of the person whom he esteems; it loses its name and its odiousness, and before you have learned all the virtues of a person of this description, you will very probably have learned to imitate some of his defects. Do not think, therefore, that you are perfectly safe with one who has many of the dispositions which qualify him for friendship, if there be a single part of his character which you cannot imitate without destroying your own virtue. I should never take a man as a bosom friend whom I could not follow into every place and copy after, or at least not be ashamed of any thing he did.

When you grow an old man like me, you will have many general acquaintances, who, instead of leading you astray, will derive benefit from your example; and you will have particular friends whom you will love with your whole heart; but, as I now suppose myself counselling young men of frank and honourable minds, your own experience will join in the observation, that there are a few steps only between the making an acquaintance and a friend. The impetuosity of youth accords ill with the moderation of age. No reasoning of mine will be competent to overcome this law of nature at this period of life; and it follows, that if you are inclined to be idle, or dissipated, or extravagant, you may find abundance of friends to suit your humours; but you will observe, at the same time, that idleness, dissipation, and extravagance, are not laws of nature. You may depend upon it, that friendship cemented by vice is founded on selfishness, and must be easily dissolved, fading away like the morning dew. It is not that generous affection which subsists between men of worth and integrity, that noble and disinterested regard for another which makes you seek his good, and desire to become one mind and one soul with him and his virtues. Therefore, if sinners entice thee, consent thou not; but meantime the friends thou hast, and whose adoption thou hast tried, grapple to thy soul with hoops of steel. One of the old English poets gives a beautiful picture of such a friendship; but as I always quote from youthful memory—for I have none now—I do not know who it is:—

> "They both were servants—they both princes were;
> If any joy to one of them was sent,
> It was most his to whom it least was meant;
> And fortune's malice between both was cross'd,
> For, striking one, it wounded th'other most."

You will often hear weak and discontented persons repeating from day to day, that friendship has left the world, and nothing but self exists in its room. The amount of this observation is no more than this—that they have never found it; and it is a sure sign that they have never deserved to find it; for whenever you inquire into these declaimers, you will find them to be peevish, selfish men, who consider friendship as a compact of advantage—a sort of unsteady men, who cannot continue long in the same mind; or vicious men, who must either debauch their friends or part with them. The friendship of selfishness, if there be such a thing in existence, endures only till one of the parties finds himself deceived; a weak mind is steady until it is engaged in forming a new friendship; and a vicious man has no reason to complain.

From all this I wish you to learn, if you desire to obtain this blessing of infinite price, that it depends on yourself whether you shall ever obtain it. If you come to the market, bring along with you the coin which will purchase the commodity. The free and uncontrolled commerce of the affections is founded on virtue; of which, if you are destitute, you have no right to blame other men for the want of friendship. Do you wish to enjoy the esteem of good men? then, make yourself worthy of it. A young man who possesses any degree of reflection and foresight, will easily see the advantage of recommending himself to the worthy by a due regard to his own character. He secures not only the approbation of his own mind and a fair reputation in the mean time, but, like a general who is beloved by his army, he is surrounded by an impenetrable host, who will repel the dangers of life, and make his passage through it safe and honourable. The love of good men is a defence to him who possesses it. It gives the whole world a favourable impression of his virtues, and it opens to him sources of advantage and improvement of which nothing but bad conduct can possibly deprive him.

Vice seeks concealment; and it is one of its distinguishing attributes, that it persuades its votaries to indulge in its practices without the fear of detection. Men's delicacy hinders them from telling you that you were last evening committing a debauch. Your own self-love will not allow you to believe that a thing is known which you wish to conceal. You do not know that the men around you contrive to look into your heart, or at least into your most secret actions; or, if the thing should be known, you flatter yourself that the apologies which you study to make for yourself are so plausible that they cannot miss to be generally sustained. But these are the dangerous rocks on which the innocence and integrity of thousands are daily shipwrecked beyond the hopes of recovery. Be not deluded: there are a thousand avenues to the heart, and to the most secret actions, through which the world obtain distorted views of your character. There is no truth of greater importance to a young man beginning life than this one which I am stating. The vain hope of concealment is often the first thing that blunts the edge of that ingenuousness which is the great guard of virtue. Be assured, then, that if men do not judge of you as you are, they will be ready to err on the uncharitable side, and make you worse rather than better. Were it even possible to deceive the quick and satirical eye of the world, your character would gain the detestable addition of hypocrisy to your other vices, and you would shun the intimacy of good men for fear of being discovered. Your connexions with the worthy are the test and security of your virtue. Cultivate their friendship, imitate their example, listen to their advice, and *if sinners entice thee, consent thou not.*

There is a wide difference between one who learns to practise a virtue and one who only affects to do it. In the one case there must be something in the soil to cherish and bring forward the infant plant— some native strength to make it rear its head during the frosts of the spring, and to secure that freshness and vigour in its whole progress which shews it to be indigenous. In the other you place a flower in a bottle, where its temporary freshness and beauty cannot conceal from you that it is not in a natural situation. There is a modesty in pure desires after excellence which affectation can never counterfeit. Na-ture has bestowed on us the power of looking behind the mask. It never costs us much trouble to discover a character, if our prejudices would let us. We see what he wishes to be, and we are informed by his awkward attempts that it is not what he really is. Affectation also gen-erally fixes on splendid excellencies for the objects of its imitation; for, when we step beyond the limits of nature, we are easily induced to aim at something conspicuous. For instance, I never knew a gentle-man in my life whom as many young friends attempted to imitate as Professor John Wilson, in his manner, speaking, and composition— not only his pupils, but long ere he was a professor, or distinguished for any thing very particularly superior; and I declare that every one of them made a fool of himself. I lectured some of our mutual friends full broadly upon this, but they denied the imputation, and said it was all jealousy, because no one attempted to imitate me save the professor himself.

But before closing this essay I must remind you that there are two classes of men who are in nothing benefited by the studies of their youth, and with neither would I wish you to form intimate friend-ships. The one class consists of those who rest their character on their conversation and manners, though every thing they say or do tells you they have learned nothing, or have taken particular good care to forget what they have learned. The other consists of those who rest their character entirely on learning, and bore you for ever with it. I advise you, both in your own character, and in the choice of your intimate friends, to avoid either of these extremes. The liberal sciences are the business and occupation of youth, but we do not acquire them merely for the purpose of displaying them. They are no farther neces-sary than to invigorate your mind and to prepare you for the dis-charge of active and important duties. The possession of learning, there-fore, is useful to your character, but never ought to be made the pa-rade of it. Consider for what it was that you were bred to virtuous knowledge, and had the germs of wisdom early implanted in your mind. It was to teach you to rule your passions, to subdue their rage, and stay their headlong course through the mazes of eventful life. Reflect, that life and death are only varied modes of endless being. Reflect, that life, like every other blessing, derives its value only from the use you make of it. It was not for itself that the Eternal gave it, but for a nobler end, and that end is VIRTUE. If your life is preserved by the loss of your wealth, the bargain is profitable, but both would be cheaply saved by the loss of virtue. Therefore, *my son, if sinners entice thee, consent thou not.*

Sermon VI

Reason and Instinct

"I pray God your whole spirit, and soul, and body, be preserved
blameless."

THIS is a difficult subject for an old shepherd to enter upon. What!
hath man a spirit, a soul, and a body? So St. Paul seems to infer, and
therefore I am bound to believe it as true; but how to separate the soul
and the spirit, I am rather at a loss. The latter I must suppose to be the
principle of animal life inherent in every living creature, and resident
in the blood and the nerves; and the other that reasonable and immortal substance in the human race which distinguishes them from all
other earthly creatures, and is the fountain of thought, reason, and
conception. It is a ray of the Divinity; a spirit united to an organised
body, by which all the operations of mind are carried on. Its existence
is apparent by consciousness or conception of our own being, and its
continuing permanent amid the successive changes of our material
frame. Philosophers have come to no certain conclusion as to its seat
in the body, with the exception of my friend and patron Dr. Dunlop,
who is quite decided on the subject,—and there are more impossible
theories, too, than his; but as it may not be deemed orthodox, I do not
choose to set it down here. The truth is, that its qualities and substance
no man can comprehend. To state any other opinions of men concerning it, would be but exposing human ignorance.

Some of the ancients have supposed that there are three kinds of
souls, the rational, the sensitive, and the vegetative. But in all ages the
soul has furnished questions of difficulty, and no human investigation
has yet proved adequate to the final settlement of the dispute; and after
all that has been written on this incomprehensible subject, the utmost
that can be inferred amounts only to this, that all we know of the soul
is merely its various states of changeful feeling. Its immortality is, I
think, manifest, from that longing after immortality inherent in every
bosom; from the apprehension of the mind when filled with remorse
on account of guilt; from the unsuitableness of the present state to the
intellectual faculties of men; and from its capacities of enjoyment, and
the ideas we are led to entertain of the Divine administration.

It appears to me to be a matter of great doubt, whether we shall most increase our knowledge respecting the residence of the soul by considering the frame and organisation of the body, or by attending to the various workings of that living principle which animates us. It is in this last way, I confess, that I have formed my notions on the subject, and they are still so indistinct, that I really cannot say whether it resides in the brain, the heart, or the muscles, or in them all together. It is too true, that the wisest of men often mistake their way in the world by thinking that their ingenuity is employed in a matter unworthy of them unless it be engaged in pursuits above human comprehension.

I shall, therefore, in treating of the human soul, attend to those near resemblances to reason and intelligence which we find in the brute creation, and consider whether our souls be different from theirs, or only superior to them. The lowest part of our rational nature, if it be a part at all, is certainly that which receives the impression of external objects. Now it is an undoubted fact, that animals of almost every description possess this faculty. They see the same objects, hear the same sounds, and enjoy the same sensual pleasures that we do; but whether such impressions are made on body or spirit, is rather a puzzling question. I believe—but, being a mere pupil of nature, am no authority to be depended on—that there is a copy of these impressions, similar to the images of mountains, rocks, and trees, reflected from a smooth lake, thrown over all creatures, both men and brutes. Now, though I believe in this, the nature of the unsubstantial copy I do not comprehend. But whenever I come to examine the uses which men and the brute creation make of the same impressions made on similar organs, I can then perceive the power of reason and intelligence in the one, and the want of them in the other. The experience of those animals which have the nearest affinity to human wisdom is varied in their different kinds, though it be nothing more than an unvaried and delegated power, the operation of which is limited to the continuation of the species, or to the preservation of the individual. I have studied the character of sundry of the most ingenious and docile animals very minutely, but have never yet been able certainly to discover any approach to amelioration, any increase of wisdom, or any addition made to the experience or instinct of any animal, in any considerable degree, when left solely to the exertion of its own powers and ingenuity. How different from this is man, who continues still increasing in knowledge, and will do world without end! I consider human life merely as an apprenticeship to immortality; and this belief has taught me, more than the reasoning of a thousand volumes, that God has bestowed on man a faculty which he never intended any other earthly creature to possess.

I have witnessed some, and read of other very remarkable instances of the combination of these impressions communicated by the organs, amounting to something very like reflection and judgment, in some animals, and like memory, in many more. I have seen a shepherd's dog contrive expedients for effecting his purpose which one-half of the human race were incapable of in the same instant of time. I have like-wise seen some extraordinary instances of recollection in horses. In-deed, they seem never to forget any incident that befalls them, nor the place where it happened. I once came to a reverend divine fairly arrested on his journey, in the middle of a wild moor, by this singular faculty of his horse. He had alighted, and was whipping her round and round, but when he saw me approaching he gave over.

"What's the matter wi' ye, Mr. Paton?" said I. "What ails ye at your yaud?"

"Why, I bogged her there the year before last, and had very nearly lost her," said he; "and she seems to have a better memory than a judgment, for though the road is now mended and firm, she will not go near it."

I could multiply hundreds of instances of the same kind, especially in dogs; and elephants, I believe, are accounted still superior. Be it so; yet I trust I shall promote the purposes of true wisdom better by tracing the great and distinguishing lines which God has drawn between man and the lower creation, than by puzzling you with a few points of resemblance, which no man can perfectly understand. There is no doubt that there are many animals which imitate, in some instances, the reason that we boast of. They can keep an object steadily in view, and they can take the nearest road to the attainment of that object.

Shall we, therefore, infer that there is an immaterial spirit in brutes as well as in men? I think there is. But it does not follow that, like the spirits of men, they shall return to God who gave them. Solomon is of the same opinion, and very explicit on this point: "Who knoweth the spirit of man that goeth upward, and the spirit of the beast that goeth downward into the earth?" I say, then, seriously, and I hope without offence, that beasts have souls; and that these souls proceed from God himself, who is the great moving spirit of the universe. In saying so, I apply the observation to the instincts which he has implanted peculiar to every species. Instinct is, I think, an impression on an animal similar to what we discover in the vegetable creation, where every seed puts forth the stem, the leaves, and the blossom, peculiar to its species. Where is the intelligence of the majestic oak or the humble shrub? yet they follow all in the same course with one another. But the power which animals have over their mind, by which they seem to recall and combine their thoughts, is certainly of a different kind, but can only be said to approach to reason because capable of improvement.

It is indeed not easy to define the precise limits between reason and instinct. The latter, in creatures so short-lived, is in many instances the more extraordinary of the two. Who teaches the new-yeaned lamb, the first minute of its existence, to seek for the dug of its dam, and never once to mistake the place where it is to be found? Who teaches the birds to build their nests of the same materials, and of the very same form and dimensions, with those of their predecessors? or the bees to construct their cells with the most mathematical exactness? The works of these little architects of nature are truly wonderful! But there is one endowment of instinct which has often amazed me most of all. The salmon-fry are bred and reared, in many instances, thousands of miles from the ocean, yet they all set out for it simultaneously at the same period. They have no guide, no director, no one to inform them that there is an ocean, without which they cannot live—nothing but that supreme power which pervades the universe, and rules and directs the motions of every living creature, plant, and flower. The more closely we study the works of nature, the more shall we admire and adore the Almighty power and wisdom that created and governs it. But these rapid and miscellaneous observations lead me now to treat the subject more philosophically.

Great men have differed so widely on this subject, that it is manifest the greater part of them have been wrong. From the resemblances which are observed between man and the brute creation, it has been the great object of philosophy to deduce their specific and leading differences; and it is astonishing how much the regard for particular theories has narrowed the understandings of men otherwise great and good. Because they have found some points in which a faint resemblance may be traced, they cannot be satisfied with the reason bestowed on them, unless there be some one thing peculiar to themselves, and in which none of their fellow-creatures of the lower orders can possibly participate. The man who pursues this one thing, whether he fixes on reason, speech, or risibility, is just exerting the powers of a rational mind to bring himself to the nearest possible level with the brute creation. On this important subject it is much more difficult to trace the resemblance than to mark the difference. The reason of brutes consists in a few efforts of memory and in a few instances of combination. This, to be sure, is wonderful, because we cannot account for it on other principles than those of immateriality. Still, they are more like the effects of varied instinct than the acts of a reasonable mind, for the efforts of such rational powers are always limited in their object. The most stupid of the feathered tribe, for example, turn the eggs daily in the nest during incubation. This seems to be the result of thought, founded on experience, and altogether necessary to maintain an equal heat. But I have sometimes thought that the great heat in the breast of the hen at that period might feel a temporary relief by turning the cool side of the egg upward. In that probable case it cannot be attributed to a principle of reason, but to one of those wise provisions of nature without which no race of animals could exist. The bee, also, in the double cells of the comb, always finishes the joinings on the one side opposite to the opening of the other. May not this also arise from the inconveniency which would otherwise be occasioned in laying the foundations of the cells? Many more examples might be extracted from nature, if we understood the principles properly which occasioned them, and might all be traced to causes equally simple, and equally unconnected with the gift of reason; and therefore it behoves us to look carefully to the various impressions made on animals, before we decide hastily on the degree of reason which people would naturally suppose they possess.

These results of impressions, if we compare animate with inanimate things, are not more extraordinary than waters sinking or trees growing upward. This investigation leads us to hesitate whenever we feel disposed to ascribe the power of reason to any of the brute creation; for when we pass the bounds of those sallies of intelligence, imperfect as well as doubtful, and begin to contemplate the vigour and power of human thought, there can scarce be room for hesitation. I therefore again repeat it, that it is infinitely more difficult to discover any resemblance to reason in brutes, than it is to shew the decided difference between their reason and ours. That animals have each a language of their own to one another, there can be no doubt. I know a good deal of their languages myself. I know by the voice of the raven when he has discovered one of my flock dead—I know also his prelude to the storm and to fine weather. The moorfowls can call one another from hill to hill. I learned to imitate their language so closely that I could have brought scores of them within the range of my shot of a morning. The blackcock has a call, too, which brings all his motley mates around him, but the females have no call. They are a set of subordinate beings, like the wives of a nabob. They dare not even incubate upon the same hill with their haughty lords. But the partridge, and every mountain-bird, have a language to each other, and though rather circumscribed, it is perfectly understood, and, as Wordsworth says, "not to me unknown." Even the stupid and silly barn-door hen, when the falcon appears, can, by one single alarm-note, make all her chickens hide in a moment. Every hen tells you when she has laid her egg; and, lest it should not be well enough heard or understood, the cock exerts the whole power of his lungs in divulging the important secret. The black-faced ewe, on the approach of a fox or a dog, utters a whistle through her nostrils which alarms all her comrades, and immediately puts them upon the look-out. Not one of them will take another bite until they discover whence the danger is approaching. If the dog be with a man, sundry of them utter a certain bleat, which I know well but cannot describe, and begin feeding again. If the dog is by himself they are more afraid of him than any other animal, and you will then hear the whistle repeated through the whole glen.

But the acuteness of the sheep's ear surpasses all things in nature that I know of. A ewe will distinguish her own lamb's bleat among a thousand all braying at the same time, and making a noise a thousand times louder than the singing of psalms at a Cameronian sacrament in the fields, where thousands are congregated,—and that is no joke neither. Besides, the distinguishment of voice is perfectly reciprocal between the ewe and lamb, who, amid the deafening sound, run to meet one another. There are few things have ever amused me more than a sheep-shearing, and then the sport continues the whole day. We put the flock into a fold, set out all the lambs to the hill, and then set out the ewes to them as they are shorn. The moment that a lamb hears its dam's voice it rushes from the crowd to meet her, but instead of finding the rough, well-clad, comfortable mamma, which it left an hour, or a few hours ago, it meets a poor naked shriveling—a most deplorable-looking creature. It wheels about, and uttering a loud tremulous bleat of perfect despair, flies from the frightful vision. The mother's voice arrests its flight—it returns—flies, and returns again, generally for ten or a dozen times before the reconcilement is fairly made up.

There is no doubt, then, that most animals have a language by which they can express their wishes and their fears to one another; but what is it compared with the extent to which the use of speech gives us access in our communications with our own species, and in managing or teaching those of the lower classes? It is rather curious, that repetition of punishment, in dogs especially, will often produce unequivocal marks of shame and regret; and a feeling of unjust punishment often affects them so deeply, that they will for a time appear quite desperate, and either lose their usual capabilities, or refuse to exert them; but the nicest attention to their actions and motives can never lead us to conclude that they possess any thing similar to the power of conscience in man. They have fidelity and attachment to their benefactors—of that there is no doubt—which sometimes exceeds the gratitude of their masters; but, then, in the one case you have facts, which you are obliged to call virtues, but in the other you have materials under the control of a reasonable agency, which are wrought up in an infinite variety of circumstances to all the virtues of which man is capable. Hence it follows, that in those instances in which brutes present to us the resemblance of reason, they are wholly destitute of what marks the interposition and power of mind. They may be wrought upon by approbation or the hope of reward from man, but in all their dealings with one another they are wholly selfish. Jealousy and revenge predominate in their natures; gratitude to one another they never think of. The instances of their ingenuity in escaping danger are astonishing; yet, except in the convolvolous doublings of the hare, I have scarcely perceived any combination of thought in preventing it.

These reflections may convince us that reason in brutes, though inexplicable to us, is limited to a very few points, connected only with their present situation, and intended by Divine wisdom to promote their safety and comfort. We see the goodness of God to his creatures, but nothing to perplex or distress us when we compare their minds with our own. I should not hesitate concerning the immortality of my own soul, though it were revealed from Heaven that the reason of beasts is the effect of organisation; nor should I abandon my hopes of immortality, though I knew that their souls were immaterial. I know and feel that there is an intelligent principle within me striving to burst the slender and corporeal boundaries by which it has pleased God to imprison and confine it. I think every man feels, or should feel, that he is possessed of an intellectual and never-dying spirit. Is it not strange, then, that we must all be trying our strength on our own nature, and, by the nicest intricacy of research, the soul of man be still trying to discover what the soul of man is? This itself is a proof of the soul's existence; but even the profound discoverer, who admits it is no nearer his purpose, nor is the wisdom of his investigation more apparent. It is still more ludicrous to think of the laborious researches which wise men have made, examining every part of the human body to discover the chief seat or residence of the soul. I say ludicrous, for I think nothing can be more absurd than to apply our notions of space to that which we allow to be spirit. I neither know, nor desire to know, where the seat of the soul is, further than that the body is the earthly palace which it inhabits during its state of probationary existence. And I have always had an idea, though I am far from pressing it on the belief of any one, that until once death was overcome, the gates of heaven were never opened to the souls of men. God himself is the food of the soul, in him alone it lives, moves, and hath its being, and can never pine for want of food, if sought in the right direction. Yet many secret indispositions and aversions to duty will steal upon it; and it will require both time and close application of mind to recover it to such a frame as shall dispose it for the pure spiritualities of religion; but it is only when our bodily eyes are finally closed that the eyes of our souls begin to see.

I shall confine myself to one or two remarks more on the impassable bourn which separates instinct from reason. Instinct teaches only the art of preservation and present comfort. But the boundaries of human thought are not confined to the trifling considerations of ease, comfort, and safety, in this mortal condition. We are partakers of the image of God, and possess the wisdom which is capable of contemplating the effects of his Divine perfections. This is the sublime faculty peculiar to the reason of man. The wisest of the inferior creation discover dread and terror when the Almighty sends forth his arrows of liquid flame, and walketh in the majesty of his thunder; but in no instance do they discover admiration. Their impressions terminate in themselves, but they give no evidence of curiosity or investigation. They feel the effect, but they neither understand nor examine the cause. It is reserved for man to look abroad into the creation, to soar above his own feelings, and from the works of God to go onward till he is lost in the splendour of his Almighty Creator. In the comprehensive grasp of reason he takes in the past, the present, and the future, possessing a commanding power over the impressions which he receives, by which he can call them up and combine them as he pleases. He sees the finger of his Maker in every leaf of the forest, in every flower of the field, and learns "to follow nature up to nature's God."

It is most distant from my intention to give you false notions of the dignity of human nature, or to cherish pride in your hearts. But the infinite difference between the soul of man and the perfections of God is sufficient for the purpose of teaching us humility. But it is a truth not to be concealed, that in the wisdom which we possess in our knowledge of right and wrong, and in our hopes of a future life, God has stamped upon us a portion of his own image, which we shall seek for in vain among the wisest and most docile of the animal creation. We perceive, indeed, the traces of his wisdom conspicuously marked out through every part of his works over universal nature. But in no other instance, except in the reason given to man, are we permitted to contemplate the perfections of the Creator, lent, as it were, to ennoble and dignify his creatures, and all the works of his hands. In all other cases we see the effects, but in this we feel the existence, of the wisdom and power of God. This of itself proves that there is a being of existence in the soul, totally distinct from every thing else within the reach of our observation in the universe.

The material frame of creation, and the changes produced on it, are regulated by the firm and established laws which the author of nature has imposed. But in that part of creation which inhabits this mortal body, we feel a conducting and governing principle which wills, and reasons, and determines, independently of all restraint, and which, therefore, I conclude to be that immaterial chain which connects us with the Eternal Spirit, and which makes us accountable to him. Rather than maintain or believe that the soul of man is the result of organisation, I would insist upon it, and with as much appearance of reason, that all changes on the material world are effected by arrangements of nature, independent of the wisdom of God—and then what would be the consequence? To a certainty, that my doctrine of materiality would lead me headlong into atheism.

It is, then, of the highest importance to us to entertain just notions of that living principle which animates and guides our conduct as rational beings. The body, which is its first residence, must soon drop into the dust; and it is not till then, as I said before, that the soul begins for herself on the face of the creation. It feels the powers of its own intelligence, and apprehends the wisdom and goodness of God. I believe, that as its clay tabernacle descends slowly and miserably to dissolution, it begins to press through the apertures of its wretched habitation, and judge for itself as mortal judgment decays; but that when the body is lifeless, when the eye is shut for ever, and all communication with external objects ceased, then that power in man which observed the works of God, and which discerned his wisdom in them, springs to a loftier and more sublime existence. Extinguished it can never be, else the Divine perfections would be confined in their operation to the narrow limits in which the soul of man is permitted to view them in this frail and imperfect state. Let us not believe it; let us not ever suppose that the organs of our mortal bodies are the only openings through which we can view the wisdom and works of God. Such a sentiment entertained is too unworthy of the great Eternal Spirit that renovates all nature.

We discover in the minutest, as well as in the most sublime parts of creation, that every motion and every change is an act of wisdom intended to promote the improvement toward perfection of the individual or of the system. We behold every where the wisdom of the means and the perfection of the end; and shall the noblest part of creation, the soul of man, formed for reflection, love, and adoration—shall this boundless capacity of human conception have been formed without an object? Shall this only part of the works of the Almighty which comprehends in its nature the ingredients of immortal life, fall like an unheeded flower among the clods of the valley, and produce no corresponding fruit? Let us entertain no such desponding thoughts as these, when every instance of Divine wisdom exhibited in this material world is a proof of our future existence. The house of this tabernacle shall indeed be dissolved, but we have before us a house not made with hands, eternal in the heavens, whose builder and maker is God.

Sermon VII

To Parents

"Train up a child in the way he should go."

THERE have been so many elaborate treatises written on education, that it will be deemed by many presumption in me to take up the theme. But, as a father, as one who has felt the want of it himself, and seen the effect of it in others, I may be allowed to contribute my mite. I am persuaded, however, that no man alive is able to set down a system that can either be agreeable or profitable to all. There has never been a system on this, or any other subject, since the building of Babel and the confusion of tongues, which has been of the least service to mankind. I would, at any rate, undertake to lead more children, and even more men, by a proverb or by a fable, than by the finest theory— so put together that the whole were fair and plausible, and the parts exactly proportioned. A man may improve a hint, but he will never do any thing more than admire a system. In some instances, this way of conveying instruction may be amusing and idle; but on the subject of education it may turn out highly pernicious. I do not speak altogether from experience, but I think, as far as morals are concerned, every thing depends upon the character of the parents and the temper of the children; and the first of these has more influence on the second than is generally imagined; and, therefore, the best system on this subject may be utterly useless to any one.

There is one rule, however, which I would give to all parents, and one which is worth a thousand volumes of speculation—and it is this. In training up a child in the way that he should go, be always yourself what you would wish your child to be. Irascibility on your part will not produce mildness or patience on his. If you are proud, you need not expect him to be humble; and if you are not economical, you may depend on it he will be extravagant. I have seen many ingenious attempts on the part of parents to retain their own vices, and yet deny the practice to their children. It will not do. The principles of religion may be inculcated to cover the deceit, but a man's vices are always better known to his family, than his virtues are to the world. It is best and safest, then, always to give a fair copy to your children, and an example every part of which it will be for their honour and profit to imitate. If you do this, a hint from you will have more influence on their minds than correction would from a parent of a different character.

A parent who is anxious for the virtue of his children should be most careful of his own; and there is no better expedient to secure and improve it, than to summon his parental affection to its support. If you were not wise enough to love virtue for its own sake, you ought at any rate to practise it, in the minutest observance of its dictates, for the sake of your children. This is one of the peculiar blessings which a parent enjoys if he will but take advantage of it; because without the danger of hypocrisy or the blame of affectation, he may train himself to virtue by habits which discover their usefulness as he continues to cultivate them. He is doubly rewarded; first in his own improvement, and then in the visible effects of his example on those who are dearest to him. Every one attaches a considerable degree of respect to the venerable name of father; and his important charge makes us bear his superior strictness and caution without envy; and we never call him precise even when he descends to the minutiæ of fair and honourable conduct. He has, then, for his own sake, and for the sake of his family, the consent of mankind to be as virtuous as he pleases.

He may always depend upon this, that children are not the last to discover the weakness of their parents. In the first stages of infancy, if you are easily provoked, they will soon find out how far they can go without danger; and if you are easily persuaded, they will tease you into a compliance with their wishes. In the first case they will soon learn to despise you, and in the second to impose on you. The weakness of your temper will be to them the seeds of vice; and what was folly in the constitution of the father will become wickedness in that of the children. Many parents flatter themselves that they will gain the love and affection of their children by indulging their weaknesses; but remember this, that in all the relations of life, the love of parents to their children only excepted, there can be no love where there is not esteem. Nature, for wise purposes, has made this exception; but we transgress her immutable laws when we expect a return of love for the same reason that we bestow it. We may just as reasonably expect that our children will not see our failings, because we are blind to theirs. The danger here can only be prevented by firmness and gentleness combined. It is impossible to say how soon your children will respect your character, if you are able to persist in the refusal of that which you do not approve of; and they will always love you if you treat them as friends. I have no objection to your having an absolute control over them. Let your word be a law irreversible, but let it be a law of kind-

ness. The infant mind will soon prove capricious if it is not steadily
directed; and it is your business never to be capricious in the direction
of it. Never explain the reasons of every part of your conduct to your
children, or try to make them comprehend the propriety and justice of
your proceeding; for this is making them parties when they should be
taught submission. But I am decidedly of opinion that every part of a
parent's conduct should be reasonable and just. It should be capable
of bearing investigation, though there be no necessity of explaining it.

What is termed crossness in children is in almost every instance the
neglected failing of the parent. It is a weakness which your indulgence
creates, and a temper of mind which manifests your own imperfections. Children know when they are under proper authority, and will
not go a second time into the fire to burn themselves. But this authority is not gained by explanations, nor yet by measures of constant
severity. How ridiculous it is to see love without bounds, and anger
without control, struggling for the mastery in the same paternal bosom!
and what good fruits can follow from injudicious indulgence and excessive severity?

But in training up a child in the way that he should go, a certain
degree of correction may sometimes be necessary; for, though I disapprove of it in general, I dare not altogether condemn it. But it ought
never to be applied in any case where a fair and honourable expedient
will answer the same end. If you wish to be feared as a tyrant, it will be
no difficult matter to force from your family the obedience and submission of slaves. It requires no more than severe chastisement to keep
alive the impressions of terror; but the consequence of this is sure to
be, that your children will not learn to distinguish between negligence
and immorality in themselves, nor between the worst passions and
virtue in you. It will oblige them always to counterfeit a character to
please you; and by thus constantly wearing a mask, they will become
hypocrites through life, or openly vicious when they are no longer
afraid of you. It is far the safest way, then, never to inflict corporeal
punishment, unless it be for vice or immorality; for this distinguishing
line in your conduct will enable them to see vice and hate it. If you
follow this rule, the defects in your children which call for correction
will occasion you more grief than anger; and no punishment has so
much effect on a young mind as that, which discovers the sorrow and
regard of the parent or teacher who inflicts it. Your reluctance demonstrates your love, and, at the same time, the nature and odiousness of
the crime for which they suffer; it both corrects them and makes them
respect you.

A person trained up with this proper hatred of vice must hate it always. There can be no situation in his future life in which cruelty, falsehood, and injustice will not deeply affect him. His power of conscience, I may say, is formed by the justice or injustice of parental correction. He learns from his infancy to be more grieved with his faults, because they will offend a friend who loves him, than afraid of the punishment to which they will subject him. How delightfully different is this feeling from that of a child whose whole manners are formed under the frown or rod of his parents, by which every thing may be corrected and yet no habit of virtue formed! You may depend on it, that those who are found constantly in the wrong, are under a regimen which will never suffer them to be right. If you can cure one defect in the habits or minds of your children in a month, you do them much more good than if you were to condemn and punish a hundred errors in a day. O, how often have I pitied the little screaming victims of parental rage, who every minute hesitated to do right lest it should be censured, and who seemed always under the influence of the same terror, whether they were stupid, or negligent, or vicious! and I have pitied the parents still more, who deemed this system the perfection of a good education. Let the recollection of punishment be always connected with the idea of vice, and you will prevent that confusion in the minds of your children, which will infallibly destroy their virtue.

It is too true that you may easily convert a fault into an immorality, by being severely strict in the tasks which you appoint; and then it becomes difficult for children to judge between negligence and disobedience. On this very point thousands of the rising generation are daily ruined. The parents begin by making negligence in this restricted sense a crime, and one that deserves punishment; then the tutor, subsequently, has scarcely another idea than to make all virtue consist in attention to his instructions, and all vice in the neglect of them. The best part of youth is spent in sowing the seeds of vanity, and the harvest afterwards is pedantry or vice. One would think, from this mode of education, that learning and taste were alone sufficient to make men humble, just, and affectionate; and that provided they know a great deal, that is, plenty of words, for which they never have any use, it is not thought of any importance although they never be taught to do any thing. You will best avoid these dangers by taking the virtues of your children into your own hands. Never trust this important part of education to your master of languages, for the copy must be set by yourself. You must hold their hand, you must praise their improvement, you must hold up to them the perfect standard which they are to imitate, if you wish to receive comfort from them, and to be honoured by them in your old age.

Every kind of learning necessary to a man's profession may in his youth be made subservient to his virtue. I do not mean that mathematical or classical studies have any thing in themselves to direct our future conduct in life, but honourable emulation, unaffected humility, and industrious habits, may be acquired, in training the mind to knowledge, with more effect than in using it to its necessary purposes after it is acquired. From this statement you will easily perceive my opinion to be, that the rod is pernicious to virtue; compulsion never forms a habit, but rather adds a disagreeable restraint to a natural aversion. The free voluntary application of the mind from generous motives is blunted, and at length extinguished by the fear of punishment; and we can never suppose that sullen submission is humility.

Since I began this essay I have perused several printed plans of education, but they are merely scenes of romance; and to train up a family by such plans is impracticable. They suppose feeling and attention on the part of parents which are not to be found in the world; and gratitude and the expression of it on the part of the peasantry in the neighbourhood, which are equally imaginary. The picture is calculated to engage the minds of the young and the sanguine. It is beautiful to read and to contemplate; but then it is overcharged and not in nature. It is in vain to look for the original; and yet those who have been accustomed to feel by representations, and to form their ideas of the lower classes from books, will be dreadfully disappointed when they come to the trial; the very coarseness of their expressions never fails to disgust a well-polished mind.

There are certain fine feelings which compel the owners to weep at a tragedy, and there are others of a more common but more delicate nature, which induce the holders to soothe the afflicted; and it is a curious fact, that can hardly be accounted for on philosophical principles, that men are most subject to the former sort of feeling, and the fair sex to the latter. This is the most beautiful and interesting trait in the character of woman; there is no scene of distress from which she will shrink, if her aid can afford any amelioration to the sufferer. This is the feeling, this is the character, which I beseech you to implant in the minds of your children from their earliest years; but as I hold it an infallible maxim that example is better than precept, if you wish to bring up your children in the way that they should go, make them acquainted with men as they are, and, at any rate, attentive to all the poor and distressed within your reach; and this will infallibly teach your children the virtue of humanity.

Notwithstanding all that has been said in the tales for children, it is the common complaint of gentlemen residing in the country, that the

poor whom they relieve are very rarely grateful for the attention paid
to them. And they say farther, that they find as much chicanery and
cunning in the humblest stations of life as they do at court. I do not
choose to enter into this, though I am rather disposed to believe, that
human nature, diversified in its modes as it is, must still be the same in
substance every where. But I am certain, if you do not think of balanc-
ing your account of kindness with gratitude received, you will infallibly be respected by your poor neighbours: the manner in which they
approach you and speak to you and of you will make a favourable
impression on the minds of your children; they will be early habitu-
ated to the modes and expressions of homely gratitude, and to respect
honesty, though it should not be dressed in a fashionable garb. There
will, doubtless, be instances in which your kindness will not be repaid
as it deserves; but you must beware of allowing the irritation of your
mind to lead you to general censure against the common ranks of
mankind in the presence of your family. Children enter more easily
into the resentments of their parents than any thing else, and if you
teach them to resent in the mass, pride and haughtiness in their future
demeanour will be the fruits of your instructions. Kindness, therefore,
to men of inferior rank, taking care to avoid every appearance of un-
due familiarity, is the true medium of conduct to steer by.

The principal use of a man of fortune and influence in society appears to me to be this very thing, to accommodate himself to the wants
and distresses of the poor and afflicted. He lives to little purpose if he
does not communicate the blessings he has bountifully received. He is
neither possessed of good taste, nor capable of happiness, if he is ignorant of the pleasure resulting from benevolence. God has distinguished
you by fortune, honour, and power, then think of the gratitude incumbent on you, and at the same time of the great good which it lies in
your power to do. Your attention to the poor will be rewarded by the
most grateful feelings of humanity, and by the dispositions and habits
which you give to your children, in training them up in the way that
they should go.

I maintain, then, as I did formerly, that good morals, good breeding, and a tendency to kindness of heart and benevolence, are the
cream and essential parts of good education. The daily repetition of
the best precepts of morality, whether they be conveyed in the shape
of a maxim or a proverb, are insufficient to form the infant mind to the
standard of parental expectation. Mankind in every period of their
existence are directed more by habit than by precept; this is a leading
truth which I have observed in myself, my brethren, and most intimate acquaintances. Man is, in fact, more the child of habit than any

other creature, and the study of it is curious and interesting. A few instances, which have come under my own observation, may be amusing to the reader, without interfering with the thread of discourse, as a parson or perhaps a dean might say.

As instances, then, children are all fond of sugar and sweetmeats, but try them with tobacco or ardent spirits, they are poison to them; but yet by habit to what a height do the passions for these arrive! I knew a man, Adam Neil, who went into Edinburgh as an apprentice to an apothecary, and his circumstances compelling him to take the cheapest lodgings he could get, he took a room above a smith's, which no other person would take, at two shillings a-week; but what with the continual pelting on the stithy, and the roar of the bellows and fire, poor Neil could get no sleep, nor, when his landlady or any other body entered the room, hear a word they said, and, in consequence, he got a habit of speaking so loud, that even in the shop his voice was heard through all the street. Every night and every morning poor Neil cursed that smithy, and his great ambition on earth was to be enabled to change his lodgings. He got at length a superior situation, and the first thing he did was to change his lodgings, and take two elegant rooms in Richmond Place, after having occupied his old room for eleven years. But the eternal clink of the smithy was wanting, and not one wink could Adam Neil sleep in his new lodgings. For seven nights he declared, in my hearing, that he did not sleep seven minutes. He said he sometimes prayed, and sometimes swore unto himself, but sleep had utterly departed from his eyes, so that on the eighth day he was obliged to go and beg his old lodgings back again, and there he still remained when I knew him, a rich, hearty, jovial, loud-speaking old fellow.

My own experience how much man is the child of habit, is more simple, but to the same purpose. I lived two years at Elibank, the most quiet and sequestered place in Scotland; from that I went to Willenslee, where a loud roaring stream ran close by the back of the stable where I lay. For a fortnight, I am sure, I did not sleep two hours, but then I made up for it by day, wrapped in my plaid, among the heather. From that, after two years, I went to another quiet remote place, but no sleep could I enjoy for many a day for want of the lullaby of Willenslee burn. There was a small burn passed at a little distance from my bed, and I was wont to raise my head and listen to the delightful hush.

Now this quality of forming the mind by habit is more visible in infancy than in any other period of life. The minds of children are not capable of reasoning on the expediency and excellency of any rule laid down. They may love virtue for its own sake, but they are not ever able to calculate on the inconveniences of to-morrow, when they are under the influence of a motive which at the present moment engrosses their attention. The most impressive discourses on the beauty of virtue are entirely unregarded by them, and yet, singular as it may appear, you will find more parents and instructors of youth attempting to reason them into goodness, than forming their habits by mild discipline and example. But this is a confession on the part of the teacher, that it is easier to point out the road than to walk in it, or perhaps it is the mere vanity of speaking about what he cannot so easily perform. But if you wish to train up your child in the way that he should go, be careful to take the path before him.

There is one thing you should always remember, that the little traits of character which are formed in youth uniformly turn out to be the virtues or vices of old age. If your children respect you for your virtues, and love you with a pure and sincere affection, you may be assured that the same affection will expand to all the connexions which they will afterward form in the world. If they are in the habit of submitting implicitly to your will without murmuring, they will be prepared to submit early and easily to all the restraints which the laws of God and man have imposed on wickedness; or, if you have accustomed them from their infancy to fill up their time in some useful and agreeable employment, they will be sober and industrious to the end of their lives. It is on this account that women, if they are not afterward spoiled by seeing too much of good company and the gay world, are more correct and delicate in their manners than men. On the other hand, if your children are impatient under disappointment, eager for happiness, but soon tired of the pursuit of it by the only path in which it is to be found—if they be fickle in their affections and ungovernable in their tempers,—you may allow your best friends to predict, that when they become men and women they will be selfish, proud, insolent, and unrestrained in their actions, and that they have not when children been trained up in the way that they should go.

Always consider, then, that on your present conduct depends the future happiness and respectability of your family. You are now training young fruit-trees to a wall, and as long as the twigs are limber and pliant, your task is easy and delightful, but if you allow them to shoot up to strong branches, you will have much to lop off; and with great labour, if you can do it at all, will you ever be able to bend or direct them to your wish. You are breeding up flowers of immortality, and what will be your reckoning at the last day if you do not train them up in the way that they should go!

Nature, for the wisest of purposes, has withheld the strong and ungovernable passions till we are approaching to manhood. It is doubt-less to give to parents who are interested in the welfare of their chil-dren a reasonable time for their instruction, and instilling right princi-ples, before the violent passions of manhood begin their powerful sway. The passions of children are indeed keen and fretful, especially if not kept under the rein, but they are much more easily restrained and governed than the unbridled passions of youth. Children are impelled by the desire of acquisition, not of enjoyment, in missing of which they feel disappointment; but no inward craving for a sinful gratifica-tion. It is obviously easy at this period of life, if you are at the pains to do it, to give the young idea any direction or habit you please; and shall you not be rewarded for your trouble, when you consider that the moderation and command of themselves which you now give them will be the best bulwark and defence against the turbulent passions which they will have to combat, and which, less or more, lie in the path of every individual of the human race?

I have now the charge of a considerable, and, I hope, amiable and virtuous family, and if I had the charge of ten, I should govern them by the simple laws which would be sufficient to direct mankind, if they were wiser and more virtuous than they are. Generosity would be the great virtue I should reward. Injustice, falsehood, cruelty, and ingrati-tude, would be almost the only crimes I should punish. With unremit-ting and steady attention to the different tempers and abilities of my pupils, I should promote in them the habits of industry, the bowels of kindness, and the virtues of patience and humility; and in every step of their progress I should teach them to love God for his goodness to the fallen race of Adam, to walk in his ways, and to understand his word.

The first principles of moral virtue being thus established in the youthful heart, I am at a great loss what plan of general instruction to recommend. I know it will be regarded by many as total want of expe-rience and discernment; but, as a pupil of nature, I must speak out my sentiments. I have a great aversion to college education; indeed, I hold it in utter contempt—and sorry am I that it should be regarded as nec-essary towards the entering on any of the learned professions; for why a young man who, by private tuition and diligence, has rendered him-self, on examination, equal or superior to any of the collegians, is not considered capable of performing the same duties, it is above my ca-pacity to comprehend. But having said thus far that I despise a college education, I must give you some reasons for it.

In the first place, then, I never saw any young men the better for it. The things taught are too abstruse for common comprehension, and altogether unsuitable to the young men, as far as I could judge, having no relation whatever to the circumstances and manner of life in which they were afterwards to be engaged. I have listened to many lectures of the most able professors, and it is perfectly obvious to me that they are of no avail whatever to the students, but just go in at the one ear and out at the other, or fall like the treasures of the sky on the firm flint. And it strikes me, that our colleges having been founded and established so long ago, they were designed purely or chiefly for the sake of that theology which was then in vogue, being either totally or in part calculated for the disputes and wranglings of divines, and of no use whatever to the lawyer or physician, and still less to the merchant and gentleman. Some of the classes bear evident marks of this design, and among them I have no hesitation in reckoning logic and philosophy. On these, I am told, nearly two whole sessions are consumed at the university, and, as far as I can judge, they must, to the greater part of students, be perfectly unintelligible; and, if they could be understood, I cannot for my life discover their use, unless it be to promote materialism, and ultimately atheism.

Nature has made all the chief pleasures of life, and all knowledge which is generally useful, easy of attainment. Would men but be at the pains to study and observe this, they would soon discover what is the sort of knowledge they should acquire and teach. But it has unluckily happened, that many who ought to have been wiser, have ever neglected that knowledge which is obvious and useful, and have puzzled their brains to unravel what is difficult, metaphysical, and useless. From the difficulty they find in acquiring it, they conclude that it must be important, and they lay out their whole exertions in delivering it to others; but if these learned gentlemen would but take a little notice of what is passing before them in the world, they would easily see the utter unprofitableness of what they magnify so much. As instances, then, I aver, that in no company of gentlemen is metaphysics or the logic of the schools ever mentioned—that no gentleman by the deepest skill in them will ever make a better figure at the bar or in the House of Commons—his eloquence in the pulpit will never be the more persuasive by the study of them—he will never understand the animal economy the better, nor will the study of metaphysics in particular ever give him a higher relish of virtue, or enable him to act with greater propriety in life.

It may be argued that these are merely aphorisms of my own; but I would like to see the man that could contradict them, and, at the same time, keep within the range of common sense. If these are admitted, then why must acquirements that are so confessedly of no use, and that are never so much as talked of in good company, waste two years of a young man's time, as well as his means, which are frequently not over-abundant? Life is not so long, nor time of so little value, that it should be consumed in useless studies, and in studies which any well-bred gentleman would be ashamed to have it even suspected that he had ever employed his thoughts about. I am sorry to say, but I am certain, that if the time some, nay, many, young men spend at the university so absurdly, in hearing crabbed questions and metaphysical jargon, were spent in the study of ancient and modern history, astronomy, and geography, they would be much better accomplished, and appear so in the judgment of every one with whom they conversed. Therefore, in training up a child in the way that he should go, I should never recommend to him the study of logic or metaphysics.

The disquisitions which I myself have heard on that grand unfathomable thing MORAL VIRTUE, appeared to me to be deplorably absurd. These disquisitions are so abstruse, and their disputes about the foundations of morality so different, that it is impossible to know who is right or who wrong; therefore, I think we may take it for granted that they are all wrong together, and not one of them is of any necessity or use. One contends that morality is founded on the will of God; another, in conformity to truth; a third, in the fitness or unfitness, or in the eternal and unalterable relations or differences of things; a fourth, in a moral sense or discernment, supposed to be natural to the human mind; another establishes his system on sympathy. Harmless but absurd principles! "Words! words!" as Hamlet says.

But the worst thing of all is, that whatever scheme the professor of moral philosophy contrives or embraces, he uses a long train of thin, metaphysical reasoning to establish that, and spends a great part of the year in laying down arguments for, and answering objections against, his particular system. These arguments may, perhaps, be very pleasing to him, and perhaps tangible, too, from long familiarity; but they are by far too subtile to be understood by his pupils, and leave no more impression on the mind than the eagle does on the air.

I wonder if ever a moral philosopher, in training up his child in the way that he should go, sent him to that class with the high sounding title and the body of air. I should think not, for I do not know an instance. I shall here put a few simple questions to that sublime class of men the MORAL PHILOSOPHERS, having an eye, meantime, for the answers from a highly-esteemed friend of my own. Might not these nice disquisitions about the foundations of morality be left out, and the students be just as knowing, as good, and as wise? Are any of them really able to comprehend such arguments, or make the least use of them? Might not the time be better spent in teaching them morality, by explaining the nature of the particular virtues? Would not this be more adapted to the capacity of the students, and incomparably more useful to them through the whole of life? Ought you not, then, to descend to that simple mode of teaching, instead of torturing the invention to establish what is of no avail whether it be established or not? There are undoubtedly many objects, the nature of which may be easily understood, although it is vain to search after their origin. What would you think of the merchant who, when he came to the mouth of a large river, should persist in not unloading his cargo until he had traced the river to its fountain?

I may be wrong, and shall be very glad to be set right; but I have come to the conclusion, that whatever be the foundation of morality, the nature of the particular virtues may easily be described. Young men are capable of understanding them, though not able to enter into the abstruse investigations about the origin of moral virtue. To know what virtue is, and to distinguish between that and evil, is useful to men in every station of life, but the subtile disputes about its origin are really out of the question. I should account the learned professor a wise man who should keep these to himself; or he might, for his own particular comfort and satisfaction, communicate all his knotty ideas to the one of his pupils who has most connexion with leading men, and has the best chance of being recommended as his successor, and who will most likely think himself obliged to be at immense labour to destroy the moral theory of his predecessor. It would, indeed, be hard to say what one duty of society, or what one office as a citizen, a student is qualified to sustain, after spending his money and the best of his life at a college.

Finally, I suspect that the whole parade of college education is a mere jumble of confusion. I am not so inveterate as Burns, who said of the students, "They gang in stirks, an' come out asses;" but I have often seen them come out so pedantic, that they were perfectly intolerable; and, save a little in the delightful studies of botany and chemistry, not one hair improved. Matters can't be otherwise; the professors are too fond of rank, and keep at too great a distance from their scholars, ever to find out the genius or particular turn of mind of any one of them, so as to discover what business will suit him, and what books he should read. And, moreover, the youths are obliged to attend far too many classes at once. I have known hundreds who attended five classes every day, and on expostulating with some of them on the absurdity of it, they said they could not help it without being obliged to remain some years longer at college. Now, is it not manifest that this must render the young men's minds one crude and unleavened mass of confusion?

In breeding up your children in the way that they should go, then, the first thing I most strenuously recommend is, the setting them a good example, and training them up in the fear, nurture, and admonition of the Lord. Teach them to know the value of a good education, and to be grateful to those who are spending their time in the improvement of their minds and morals; to correct all the irregularities of their temper by the sweet influences of Christian charity; to be respectful to their superiors, kind to their inferiors and equals, and benevolent to all mankind; and both the blessing of the Almighty, and the respect of their brethren of mankind, will accompany them all the days of their lives.

Sermon VIII

Virtue the Only Source of Happiness

"Happy is that people whose God is the Lord."

ALL mankind are posting on in search of happiness both in this life and that which is to come, and all taking different routes to find it; but if they would keep this maxim of the Psalmist engraved on their hearts, to take the Lord only for their God, they would be so directed that they could not miss it; but we have so many idols of ambition in this world, that, alas! how few of us take the Lord solely for our God, and his blessed word for our rule and direction. In a great city, on a Sabbath-day, it is matter of serious contemplation to see all the people posting away, with serious faces, seeking the road to heaven, and all going different ways to find it. It is piteous to hear certain sectarians preach and believe that there is no salvation to be had out of their own community. I pity all such followers of the meek and lowly Jesus; for if we seek him with all our hearts, according to the monitor which he has placed in every human bosom, then we are all flowers of the Almighty's garden, and though of different hues, shall all bloom together with him in Paradise.

In revolving in my mind this grand subject of universal pursuit, I have often been led to think that there is more written upon it, more rules laid down, and more avenues opened, than were actually necessary to direct the whole human race to the grand summit of their wishes. And yet I don't know how it is, but in my long journey through life, I have scarcely met with any man who was fully content with his condition, and who did not think he had greater cause of complaint than rejoicing. Man is a strange compound of vanity and selfishness. There is no deception which we more generally practise than that of trying to appear easy and comfortable in our circumstances, and yet there are no topics so generally expatiated on as our vast disappointments, misfortunes, and afflictions. What can be the source of these conflicting elements in the human composition? for that they really exist is quite apparent. The truth is, that man, with all his great capabilities, is a perplexed knot, which it is impossible to untie.

There are, I acknowledge, a sufficient store of evils in every man's life to embitter his comfort and to poison the springs of his enjoyment.

Were the nauseous draught to remain always on the palate, no man could be happy. Were we always to reflect on them, it were impossible that any splendour of situation, or abundance of comforts, could counterbalance the probable impending strokes which tomorrow, or at most, in some few years, may humble us to the dust, separate us from our friends, or visit us with some of the thousand ills that flesh is heir to.

But the human mind is so peculiarly framed as to forget the past, and conceal the future; and were it otherwise, it would be in vain either to speak or think of human happiness. The wisdom of Divine Providence is conspicuous in adapting our habits of thought and reflection to the situation in which we are placed. Thus, no experience of danger, no reflection on past suffering, nor even the assurance that our death must necessarily happen in a few years, can hinder us from enjoying the present moment.

Before proceeding further, I must lay it down as a first principle, that those pursuits and enjoyments which are best calculated to promote our happiness are within the reach of every man, and that the whole art is to be able to seize upon and improve them. The precarious subsistence of a child of Providence does not destroy his contentment and happiness, and the greatest abundance of the rich does not moderate their desires. A man's happiness does not at all consist in the multitude of the good things which he possesses. We have no need to apply the colouring of language in comparing the affluence of the nobleman with the simple enjoyments of the peasant. The scene is every day exhibited to our view, and we cannot withhold our senses from perceiving, that nature has provided the means of contentment in the humblest conditions of life. Some may imagine, and many do imagine, that those who are placed in mean and inferior stations must be miserable, seeing the ease and plenty of the rich around them. But the case is for the most part reversed, and we often find more genuine and unaffected happiness in the cot than in the palace.

For upwards of twenty years I have mixed with all classes of society, and as I never knew to which I belonged, I have been perfectly free and at my ease with them all. But I have always been suspicious of the happiness of the great. We only see the favourable side of things there, that side which vanity tempts them to display; but in the shepherd's cot we see nature pure and unsophisticated, and all the kindly affections of the human heart freely given vent to; and whether it be that my best days were spent among the shepherds—the days of youth, love, and gaiety, the reflection on which is delightful—I know not, but I have always looked on them as the most happy of any. They have none of the jealousies or incumbrances of the higher rank. Theirs is a state of narrow independence, fluctuating indeed, but then they know very early each year what their income will be, and rule their family expenses accordingly. The shepherd is moreover the ward of Heaven, and he knows and feels it, and bends always with a composed submission to the decrees of Divine Providence. That daily feeling naturally impressed on his mind, that all his comforts are entirely in the hand of Him that rules the elements, contributes not a little to that firm spirit of devotion for which the Scottish shepherd is distinguished. I know of no scene so impressive as that of a family sequestered in a lone glen, during the times of the winter storms and floods; and where is the glen in the kingdom that wants such a habitation? there are they left to the protection of Heaven, and they know and feel it. Nothing is to be seen but the conflict of the elements, nor heard but the raving of the storm. Then, before retiring to rest, he kneels, with all his little dependent group around, and commits himself and them to the protection of Heaven; and though their little hymn of praise can scarcely be heard by themselves as it mixes with the roar of the tempest, they never fail to arise from their devotions with their spirits cheered, and their confidence renewed, and go to sleep with an exaltation of mind of which kings and conquerors have no share. There is a sublimity in the very idea. There they live, as it were, inmates of the cloud and the storm; but they stand in a relationship to the Ruler of those which neither time nor eternity can ever cancel. Wo to him who would weaken the bonds with which true Christianity connects us with Heaven and with one another!

In taking a general view of the conditions of the rich and the poor, we see the former look with contempt on those pure and simple enjoyments of nature, or perhaps a kind female heart may feel regret for them; but they are beyond the reach of such; they never can taste them. But the poor man can witness all the preparations for a great man's table, and the infinite multitude of his comforts, without either envy, or reflection on the providence of God, but is rather disposed to pity them. Let no one, then, estimate the amount of a man's happiness by the extent of his riches and enjoyments, but rather try them by the rule of inverse proportion. Depend on it, happiness is nearest to those who are least distracted by a multitude of wants.

I believe that no man with a very large fortune or estate can be truly happy. It is a strange enigma, but it is true, that he feels no wants but the want of happiness in those very blessings which other men covet. I believe that the nobleman is happier than his sovereign; I believe that the farmer is happier than his lord; and I believe that a truly virtuous servant is the happiest of all.

The principal reason for this seems to be, that what costs us dearest we are sure to estimate highest. We receive the choicest gifts of Providence with indifference unless they are obtained with difficulty. The sweetest dishes, the richest wines, the softest beds, cloy the appetite, unless they are obtained with some difficulty,—nay, *only* cloy the appetite and fatigue the senses of him who can always procure them. There is infinitely more enjoyment in that state in which relaxation is festivity, in which the coarsest food has the seasoning—and in this rests happiness. Now, in this particular the poor man has greatly the advantage over the rich, who has no occasion and is under no obligation to labour. He has certain stated periods, after short intervals, at which his enjoyments return; and they are the sweeter, that he has laboured to procure them. This is happiness which never cloys, which brings along with it its full measure of contentment, and which does not distract its possessor, either by a multitude of objects or by unsubstantial hopes.

A man born to a large fortune has his relish for true enjoyment corrupted from his infancy. He has no restraints on his pursuits after happiness, except those which convince him, at the same time, that it is not to be found. His extensive possessions only diminish hope, without supplying contentment. We ought, then, to deliberate calmly and seriously, whether it would add to our comforts to have every wish of our hearts gratified as soon as it is formed. Let us consult our reason and experience, and say whether disappointment in some things, and expectation in others, are not necessary ingredients in human happiness. The more that fortune places us above danger and want, the less qualified are we to enjoy her favours. Abundance may increase, but never can remove chagrin and disappointment; it even makes them more intolerable in proportion as we might have avoided them, while the ease with which we may command enjoyment, opens to us endless prospects of pleasure, which we can never realise. Virtue and truth, and taking the Lord for our God, are the sole guides to genuine happiness.

The text contains very much in it; no less than the whole range of religion, virtue, and philosophy. But the latter, in my opinion, would have gained a more important end, and furthered the two former more, if it had given us the history, instead of the speculations, of the philosopher. Would it not be better if the authors on this subject were to furnish us with the pictures of their own mind and the sources of their own comforts, rather than fix on any one thing in which they fondly suppose happiness to consist?—because, if they are not happy, why should they write on it? When a man tells me that true felicity consists in the abundance of the possessions of life, he gives me no other information than that he is poor and discontented. If he places it in the sweets of pure and disinterested friendship, he has either been unfortunate in the choice of his friends, or did not deserve the friendship of the good. If he places it in the joys of requited love, he only lets me know that he is either a monk or a wretched old bachelor, who regrets the loss of pure female affection, vanished for ever. Rely, then, on this—that if fair virtue be not the theme of his commendation, he can never direct you on the way to happiness; for he himself hath never found it,—he only knows what it is to be miserable by the stings of a troubled conscience for virtues neglected, religion despised, and felicity lost.

This great chief good, then, which we all labour so eagerly to obtain, is as common as the water we drink, the air we breathe, or the most common food that supports us. It is to be found in every station of life, and neither poverty, nor pain, nor sickness, can deprive us of it; nor can a prison keep it out; nor have crowns nor palaces any thing in themselves by which they can let it. We find the human mind naturally disposed to enjoy happiness in the most trying circumstances; even the scaffold and the stake are dreadful only when painted in imagination, the suffering being then contrasted with the enjoyments which we wish not to relinquish, or with the prospects which fancy has decked out in her gayest colours. But how often has the guilty met the stroke of inevitable death without shrinking, the penitent with patience and resignation, and the martyr with joy! Yet, if it be true that a contrition without hope does not invariably depress the mind, it may be granted, on the other hand, that circumstances the most favourable, and prospects the most flattering, cannot always produce cheerfulness and contentment; but, on the contrary, we are so much the creatures of our own feelings, that, without pretending in the least to be paradoxical, I think, as formerly hinted, that ease and plenty and rank are the greatest enemies to true happiness. It is that fleeting shadow which eludes the grasp of him who seems to have it in his power, while it so frequently lurks unseen, though not unfelt, around the cold hearths of the poor and the unfortunate. It is far easier to acquire the virtue of contentment with little than with much; for God, in his all-wise providence, frequently gives a large share of temporal blessings only to shew their vanity. Let those contradict me who build houses and plant vineyards, who lay house to house, and field to field, and who withhold nothing from the capricious cravings of their appetites. Alas! their condition both in life and death testifies how little all earthly substance is calculated to insure happiness here, or direct us in the way to it hereafter. It is all vanity and vexation of spirit; and the words and the reflections of the wise man are literally true– "I hated all my labour that I had taken under the sun, because I should leave it to the man that shall be after me; and who knows whether he shall be a wise man or a fool? For God giveth to a man that is good in his sight wisdom and knowledge and joy; but to the sinner he giveth travail to gather and to heap up, that he may give to him that is good before God." "There is one alone, and there is not a second; yea, he hath neither child nor yet is there end of all his labour; neither is his eye satisfied with riches, neither saith he, For whom do I labour and bereave my soul of good? This is also vanity; yea, it is a sore travail."

Take, then, the great King of Israel as a monitor. Who ever acquired such riches, glory, and extent of dominion, as he? And yet he declared them all to be vanity and vexation of spirit; and so it will ever prove to him who spends his whole life in the pursuit, and never thinks of the enjoyment. Perhaps Solomon by this time foresaw the ruin of all the great things he had done, and the partition of his empire; since, notwithstanding the wives, concubines, and virgins that he had, he left but one son, and he was a fool.

But I have still a greater than Solomon, to whom I must now appeal. Our blessed Lord and Saviour began his moral instructions to men, by giving definitions of happiness, and shewing where it is to be found. He confines it, indeed, to no condition of life; his views are new and extraordinary; but they decisively demonstrate his knowledge of the human heart, and the abundance of that wisdom of God that dwelt in him. His instructions are, Be detached from the world, be humble, be meek, be just, be merciful, be pure, be patient, and you will be happy. These virtues are confined to no situation; they are the sources of internal peace, and he connects them with the prospects of eternity.

We have thus seen that happiness is more generally diffused, and more easily secured, than those who pursue it too keenly imagine. There is a predisposition to it in the minds of most men, which is defeated only by their eagerness to obtain it: it is good for a man to be employed in a virtuous or even trivial pursuit; but let him never be employed in the pursuit of happiness, for this gift of Heaven can only be found in the enjoyment of the present moment. If we run after it, we not only make this melancholy confession, that we are not in possession of it, but we shew that we are not likely to be so. The question, then, to every man is, not whether he looks forward to something unattained as the foundation of his comfort on earth, but if he is to be happy at all–whether there is something in his active duties to fill up his time, and something in the blessings which he enjoys to soothe and charm his mind in his present condition. This is actually that good which he can find under the sun; and if any additional comfort shall intrude itself on the plan of his life, he will enjoy it the more for not expecting it. Solomon's moral philosophy is to me better than the whole that has been produced since; and it is long since I had it all by heart. The following maxim is three times repeated, nearly in the same terms, in his works: "There is nothing better for a man than that he should eat and drink, and that he should make his soul enjoy good in his labour. This also I saw, that it was from the hand of God."

I am far from recommending to any one that insipid indifference of mind which enjoys not pleasure, or that apathy which regards not pain; for this indolence of mind is happiness without enjoyment. I consider a certain keenness of disposition, prompting to the most active exertions, as the first ingredient in the happiness of man. Whoever possesses this sort of temper, I advise him to plant, to sow, to read, write, publish—even though it were sermons; to build, hunt, angle, travel, or sail—in short, to do any thing to keep his mind engaged; but never to hunt after happiness, or set the ardour of his mind upon that. In all the other pursuits he may find a share of happiness; but by herself she is not to be caught: as well may we loose a pack of hounds to hunt the eagle. But make the Lord your God. Bow to his will in all things, and take his word for the rule of your life, and you shall be happy.

Were I to give you a philosophical definition of the word happiness, I would say that it is the mind and the object in full possession of one another. A man's life will be always pleasant, if he enter with all his heart and soul into the concerns of it. "Whatsoever thine hand findeth to do, do it with all thy might; for there is neither knowledge nor device in the grave whither we are all hastening."

But remember this is the ardour of pursuit which I recommend, not the keenness of enjoyment. I only say, that in virtuous and active engagements you will find happiness where you never expected to find it. Almost without your knowledge, the means will be connected with the end, and you will gain the prize before you have reached your imaginary goal. Take an example from childhood, which is allowed by all to be the happiest period of life. If this be true, it is merely on account that children find an object of pursuit in every thing that presents itself, and then they pursue it with such ardour! If men choose to take the same road, they will continue the happiness of childhood to their latest years, with the additional satisfaction which the choice of reason and the approbation of conscience will impart. But the minds of children are free and light as air, and with them no care obtrudes itself on an anxious heart; the pains of yesterday leave no impression, and to-morrow is an hundred years before. Did you ever hear of a man in a fox-chase thinking of yesterday or to-morrow? Let us, therefore, be engaged in the chase of wisdom and the chase of virtue. Let our duties, our actions, and our amusements, still be the objects of our eager pursuit; and, with the Lord for our God and guide, we shall never be unhappy.

There is a nice combination of activity and indifference, which, when acquired by due attention, or mixed up in the constitution, forms, perhaps, the very height of human felicity; at least, it contains the ingredients which, if well used, compose it. It consists of activity in the pursuit and indifference to the object. It gives the good in hand without the danger of disappointment; and consists of eagerness and ardour without anxiety. This state of mind is the power of seizing the happy moment at once, without waiting till time shall wear away the traces of sorrow. This seeming contradiction is easy to him who suppresses vain hopes, and who derives from every duty and occupation of life the sum of what it can give.

It is a melancholy truth, that in our character, the fancy and imagination which painted the delights of the future scene embitter the present moment. If we had not overlaid the picture with too much high colouring, we might have enjoyed life as it is. We should have learned in this checkered scene to extract sweet from bitterness, instead of rejecting the cup, because the ingredients in it are not mingled to our taste; but energy in our pursuits destroys the illusions of imagination, and never fails to direct us at last to the right goal.

With God all things are possible; and if, on one hand, the vanity of riches is illustrated by the miseries of the rich, on the other, it happens, perhaps, once in a hundred years, that a singular character gives us a conspicuous example both of the use and enjoyment of riches, in securing his own happiness and promoting that of others. But, without all doubt, happiness is most frequently found, and most sweetly enjoyed, where the curse and bitterness of plenty have never been known by experience; therefore, it is better to seize on it when we can, than to be disappointed when we think we have it in our power.

But hope, blessed hope, is still the polar star that points the way to happiness; for there is no doubt that every earthly thing is more delicious in the prospect than the enjoyment; and this delightful beacon shines for ever before the eye of the soul, burning brighter and brighter to the last, and brightest of all on the verge of the grave. I consider that all our enjoyments would be nothing if we were deprived of hope. It is the distinguished and peculiar gift of God to man—a gift which confers present enjoyment, while the blessing is in expectation. Think of the poet, the artist, the player, and many others, how they feed on the ambrosia of hope! and, after all, they derive much more pleasure from this feast of the imagination, than they are hurt afterward by the disappointment of their hopes. It is a melancholy want of fancy to build your castle on one cloud–to fix your sole attention on one object, and yet to be miserable because you cannot vary the picture which your imagination had painted.

But allowing that the approach of old age weakens the imagination and destroys the illusions of fancy, yet I am not the less persuaded that it is more possible to be contented with disappointed hopes, than with disappointment in enjoyment. It is more pleasant in any stage of life to be satisfied with little, than to be so unfortunate as to have possessions which cannot satisfy you. The brow of an old man is generally clouded in proportion to his riches. This is a great evil under the sun. Along with the infirmities incident to the last stage of life, a rich man has the melancholy want of relish for all the blessings which his fortune should procure; every thing is wrong and out of place; every body around him is to blame; and the man is miserable. He has the means but not the power of enjoyment. He has found what the world is on trial, and complains of it with disgust.

But if riches bring no corresponding enjoyment equal to the expectation, how does it happen that so many are in the anxious and unremitting pursuit to have the greatest share of them? The answer is easy and obvious. In every station we think that we may be, or ought to be, happier than we are. Nothing being more likely to realise the scenes of bliss which we fancy in prospect, than abundance of the things which we want, it is quite natural to covet and pursue the riches by which they may be acquired. Miserable beings that we are! we never know that we are pursuing a shadow until we try to grasp it, and find we have nothing. Alexander wept when he had no more worlds to conquer; and, on the same principle, the rich man is unhappy because he has every thing to enjoy, and nothing to expect.

I am an old man, and, of course, my sentiments are those of an old man; but I am not like one of those crabbed philosophers who rail at the state which they cannot reach; for in sincerity of heart I believe that hitherto no man has enjoyed a greater share of felicity than I have. It is well known in what a labyrinth of poverty and toil my life has been spent; but I never repined; for when subjected to the greatest and most humiliating disdain and reproaches, I always rejoiced in the consciousness that I did not deserve them. I have rejoiced in the prosperity of my friends, and have never envied any man's happiness. I have never intentionally done evil to any living soul; and knowing how little power I had to do good to others, I never missed an opportunity that came within the reach of my capacity to do it. I have not only been satisfied, but most thankful to the Giver of all good, for my sublunary blessings, the highest of all for a grateful heart that enjoys them; and I have always accustomed myself to think more on what I have than on what I want. I have seen but little of life, but I have looked minutely into that little; and I assure you, on the faith of a poet and a philosopher, that I have been able to trace the miseries and mis- fortunes of many of my friends solely to the situation in which they were placed, and which other men envied; and I never knew a man happy with a great fortune, who would not have been much happier without it. Nor did I ever know a vicious person, or one who scoffed at religion, happy. He goes always on from bad to worse; and I was sorry to find in the metropolis so many of a wretched set of politicians not only deists but gross blasphemers. O, my soul! come not thou into their secret; into their assembly, mine honour, be not thou united. Finally, without virtue there can be no true happiness; and if ever there was a light kindled to direct man to happiness, both here and hereafter, it is the divine revelation. Happy is that people whose God is the Lord.

Sermon IX

Marriage

"It is better to marry than to burn."

THERE are two sides of the question to be examined here; more particularly as one part of Scripture is often at a little variance with another part in this respect. Such as, "He that marrieth doth well; but he that marrieth not doth *better*." "Marriage is honourable," &c. "Whosoever findeth a wife, findeth a good thing." The apostle ought to have made some exceptions here. But I think, if every marriage were gone about prudently and regularly, with the consent of parents and friends, very few marriages would turn out to be unhappy. It is a curious fact, that throughout the whole Scriptures of truth I have never been able to discover a single hint that children had a right to marry without the consent of their parents. It was a good law; and, though our dramatists and novelists have set it sore aside by their representations of cruel and unreasonable parents, I find that, in all my experience, and the history of the world from its beginning, that these irregular marriages never have thriven. It was these which caused the destruction of the old world. They proved a grief of mind unto Isaac and Rebecca. They brought the patriarch Judah into great trouble and iniquity. They proved a grievous curse on David; and rent the kingdom of Israel from his grandson by Solomon's unlawful marriage. But even the simple register of all the evils which have sprung from rash and illegal marriages would fill many volumes.

I shall then set out by stating my own opinion frankly, that if, as in this country, every man have his own wife, and every woman her own husband, that marriage is the best institution under heaven. I have now tried both ways a long time, and my opinion ought to be of some avail; but I must likewise quote the sentiments of a far greater man, who shall for the present be nameless.

"You tell me in yours, that man and wife are one flesh. I deny it; for how can they be one flesh, and have different souls? which they have with a vengeance. The love which excited the union is soon converted into disgust. Woman is a composition of so much versatility, that she may shew an agreeable outside to the world, and quite the reverse of the picture to the man of her choice. Agreeable to the primeval curse, her desire is, indeed, to her husband; but it is a desire to torment and vex him. She has the power of speech, but not the gift of understanding. Nature has placed her in a state of subordination, and her whole endeavour through life is to attain absolute power and authority. Her charms give the first sway over the hearts of her captives, and her empire is afterwards maintained by the most unhallowed means."

How shall I answer this gentleman? I will do so by saying that his impertinence is intolerable; and it appears to me a species of ridicule with which ignorance defames the happiness it can no longer enjoy. If any man feel that he has reason to complain of woman, I request him to look for the causes of his disappointment and affliction in his own conduct; and I am much mistaken if he do not find them there.

Women are formed for attachment. Their gratitude is unimpeachable. Their love is an unceasing fountain of delight to the man who has once attained it, and knows how to deserve it. But that very keenness of sensibility which, if well cultivated, would prove the source of your highest enjoyment, may grow to bitterness and wormwood if you fail to attend to it or abuse it. I know some men who, when soliciting a favour, and when even denied it, and sore disappointed, will yet bear patiently and quietly with the pride, the haughtiness, and the ill-humour of the person who is able to confer it; and yet the same men will irritate the sensibility and wound the feelings of those tender friends who hold in their hands their happiness for life.

There lies much, indeed, in making choice of a woman worthy of your esteem; but, at all events, endeavour to make her so; and the best way to do it is to make yourself worthy of hers. Your interest and your happiness require that you should appear amiable and respectable in the eyes of your wife; and you will love her, independently of any other consideration, for the love she bears to you. This is the whole mystery of the union; and it is much easier to comprehend than it is to overstrain and keep up the mind to that high stretch of imaginary feelings with which the union at first commences. If you wish to obtain from this lasting union the satisfaction which it can bestow, you must endeavour, as I said, to conceive your wife worthy of your esteem. If any demon, envious of human felicity, should whisper that she is not so, spurn the idea, and lay not the deleterious unction to your soul.

It is not at all improbable that you may discover defects in her temper and character which love concealed from you before marriage. But remember that it may be your own fault that something substituted in place of that love has not concealed them. Still you may think for a while that it is impossible to shut your eyes against certain weaknesses and imperfections of character, either on the one side or the other; but it is to the husband I write at present; and I say, if it is impossible to shut your eyes to imperfections, surely it is not impossible to open them to gratitude, esteem, and attachment; and proper conduct on your part will secure these from the woman of your choice. It is too common to see a man of great and shining abilities selecting his friends, both male and female, from those only who pretend to admire his character. This is a weakness in human nature which can never be overcome; and is often of great value in the literary world, where many an author has nothing else to carry him forward save the approbation of a few friends.

But in marriage this is a serious consideration. It is not the girl who pretends to be enraptured with your poem in her album—with your pleading at the bar—or your discourse from the pulpit—whom you ought to choose; for in these instances it is generally all pretence with them; and they just admire you in proportion as you pay attention to themselves.

But it should always be remembered that the union of marriage is one that must continue until one of the parties shall drop into the grave. There are many instances, I fear, where convenience, to the one party or the other, is the sole inducement; but, in most cases, it is begun with mutual feelings of esteem and affection. The declaimers on this topic—that is, the disappointed—never fail to cry out that innocence and beauty are prostituted for gain, if there is much inequality of years or circumstances. Even deformity, they say, will not stand long in the market, if it has the appendage of an estate; and that wealth, though in the possession of old age, and acquired by doubtful circumstances, has the command of beauty, youth, innocence, and virtue. This I always regard as a distorted representation of the loveliest forms of our nature, suggested by disappointment and malice, without any truth or probability to support it.

I can easily understand that a woman may be deceived by the ease and splendour which wealth and independence give to the exterior of her admirers; but it is impossible for me to believe that the frankness and generosity of that charming sex will ever permit them to sacrifice their feelings to their convenience. And I have often remarked, that such marriages as were deemed a little selfish by the world were the most regularly happy of any.

Women may be deceived by appearances, or by the importunities of their aged relations; but they will never enter into the holy state of marriage when their affections are not engaged. All conjugal felicity is built on this foundation; and if it is not your own fault, you may rear a superstructure upon it which will last the whole of your life. Although there should not be that ardent and enthusiastic love which poets so fervently describe previous to marriage, or for a short time after the union has taken place, yet you may be assured, a man would not risk his happiness without esteem, nor a woman without affection. There must be something either in the character or good qualities which has brought the parties together. In the country parts of Scotland such a thing as an unhappy marriage is not known.

This induces me to believe that the greater number of marriages are infinitely happier than those who never tried the state will allow. Can we conceive any condition in which there is a fairer chance of happiness? in which friendship is so firmly cemented? in which hope is so sweetly excited? and in which so many tender relations rise up around you to fill and to expand the human heart?

"Yes, Mr. Shepherd," says the cynical unmarried man, "you, indeed, shew us the remote objects of a landscape—so remote that no person has ever discovered them before; but bring us nearer home, if you please, to the houses and firesides of this happy junction of hearts, and what do you find there?" In the little acquaintance I have had with the world, I have calculated that where there was one really unhappy junction, legally and decently made, there were at least a hundred happy ones; so that the lottery of marriage can never be a dangerous one when there are so many prizes for one blank.

The education, the character, the temper, and the original design of woman contradict every part of the supposition that the generality of the sex are troublesome and pestiferous in their disposition. I maintain that the virgin love of woman is the dearest and sweetest gift that Heaven can confer on man; and his is the blame who possesses it, if the garland do not remain green and blossom for ever.

We are bound to admire the incessant care of parents to instruct their daughters, from their infancy, in all useful and substantial acquirements. The experience of the mothers, especially, teaches them to distinguish between petty forms, which captivate and allure the trifling part of our sex, and the dignified manners which charm the wise. What pains have I seen bestowed on the infant mind to convince the dear child—the mother, perhaps, of the future hero, the poet, or the divine—that the charms of person and of dress were never once to be compared with the improvement of the mind! And it is, moreover, a common and good rule, in the education of all female children, to make them clean and neat in their person, and easy and agreeable in their manners, without making them vain.

If we look into the female mind, we shall find virtues of a brighter hue, though not of the same colours, of which we boast. We have greater depth of investigation; they, greater acuteness of perception. Our strength of mind is compensated by their liveliness. If we have more courage to brave danger, they have far more fortitude to meet distress. Our eloquence has more force; theirs has more persuasion. Their virtues are feminine, but as substantial and as useful as ours. The Author of our nature, in his infinite wisdom, has fitted the several virtues to the station which he has intended the possessors of them to occupy; and they are so well fitted to it, that you never hear women rail against the married state as unmarried men frequently do. Gentleness and forbearance are so sweetly tempered and mingled in their constitutions, that they bear the hardships of their lot, however peculiarly severe it may be, without repining or levelling a satire against such as are, by the generality of their sex, regarded as more fortunate.

That we do not, in every instance, find this intimate union productive of the greatest happiness, is either because we form engagements for life with too little consideration, or are careful to conceal the defects of our temper before marriage, and allow them to break out after; else we may suppose that there is some speck of infirmity, some pollution in the spring of all human enjoyment.

But we must take human life as it is, and not as the imagination may paint it. The scenes of delight which we figure to ourselves are nothing more than waking dreams. They are the sweet, but not quite the harmless, illusions of fancy, which, the more they are indulged in, will lay up a greater store of irksome feelings and disappointed hopes for the future part of our lives. In compensation for the loss of this happiness, which in youth we are so ready to paint on a cloud, my experience bids me assure you that the ingredients of human comforts, rising out of the different scenes of life, are totally distinct from the pictures of the imagination; yet a wise and discreet man may find them every where.

Good temper and gentleness I consider as the main avenues leading to mutual enjoyment. They meliorate the violence of contention, keep alive the seeds of harmony, and renew endearment. Banish gentleness from your hearth, and what sort of society will remain?—the solitude of the desert were preferable to it. Is it not strange, that two people, having the same common interest, should ever concur in defeating it? They must abide by, and suffer with, one another; and since nature has already provided a sufficient quantity of unavoidable evils for the state of man from without, why should he endeavour to increase them by strife within? The sense of duty and common happiness is surely of itself sufficient to recommend this virtue. It prepossesses and wins every heart, and persuades when every other argument fails. To gentle behaviour, the world is generally disposed to ascribe every other good quality. There are other good qualities which reach us not; but of the influence of gentleness, not only the partner of our bosom, but all around us partake, and therefore all love it. Its influence on our internal enjoyment is, moreover, certain and powerful. That inward tranquillity which it promotes is the first requisite to every pleasurable feeling. It is the calm and clear atmosphere, the serenity and sunshine of the mind; and when benignity and gentleness reign within, we are always in least danger of being ruffled from without.

Gentleness, sweet gentleness! it will always prove itself the most blessed guest that attends your hearth, and the balm of connubial love. With it your days will flow in a placid tenour, and you will regard every failing in others with an indulgent eye. You can retreat into the calmness of your spirit as into an undisturbed sanctuary, and enjoy, as it were, a prelude to heavenly bliss; whereas, if no attention be paid to the government of the temper, a meetness for heaven can never be acquired, and the regenerating power of religion on the soul never known. If we have none of that forbearance toward those who are nearest and dearest to us, which we all so earnestly entreat from Heaven, can we look for clemency or gentleness from the Judge before whose tribunal we and our wronged friends must meet?

Being a layman, I do not wish to enter deeply into the mysteries of religion; but I would always keep it in view. Now, a holy calmness of temper will most of all be promoted by frequent views of those great objects which the religion of the meek and lowly Jesus presents. We shall learn to look upon this world as a state of passage, and inhale the prospects of a blessed immortality—as only acting now, under the eye of God, an introductory part to a more important scene; and, elevated by such sentiments, our minds will become calm and sedate; the spirit of true religion will remove us to a distance from the grating objects of worldly contention, and teach us to bear with one another, and love one another; for the love that cometh from above is gentle and easy to be entreated;—and, in one word, the tenour of manners which the gospel enjoins when it commands us to bear one another's burdens; to rejoice with those who do rejoice, and weep with them that weep; to please every one his neighbour for his own good; to be kind and tender-hearted, pitiful and courteous; to support the weak, and to be patient towards all men;—the fruits of this spirit are meekness, gentleness, and long-suffering.

All the virtues of domestic life are lessons which are taught in the

Christian school. It is like the sun, who, though he regulates and leads on the year, dispensing light and life to all the planetary worlds, yet disdains not to cherish and beautify the flower which opens its bosom to his beam; so the Christian religion, though chiefly intended to teach us the knowledge of salvation, and be our guide to happiness on high, yet also regulates our conversation in the world, extends its benign influence to every circle of society, and peculiarly diffuseth its blessed fruits in the paths of domestic life.

The exaltation of the fair sex in the eyes of ours being my sole motive in this essay, I cannot close it better than by an extract from Irving—the most delicately and affectingly beautiful of any thing that ever was written on the female character. "Man is the creature of interest and ambition. His nature leads him forth into the struggle and bustle of the world. Love is but the embellishment of his early life, or a song piped in the intervals of the acts. He seeks for fame, for fortune, for space in the world's thought, and dominion over his fellow-men. But a woman's whole life is a history of the affections. The heart is her world; it is there her ambition strives for empire; it is there her avarice seeks for hidden treasures; she sends forth her sympathies on adventure; she embarks her whole soul in the traffic of affection, and if shipwrecked, her case is hopeless, for it is a bankruptcy of the heart.

To a man the disappointment of love may occasion some bitter pangs: it wounds some feelings of tenderness, it blasts some prospects of felicity; but he is an active being; he may dissipate his thoughts in the whirl of varied occupation, or may plunge into the tide of pleasure; or if the scene of disappointment be too full of painful associations, he can shift his abode at will, and, taking as it were the wings of the morning, can fly to the uttermost parts of the earth.

But women's is comparatively a fixed, a secluded, and a meditative life; she is more the companion of her own thoughts and feelings; and if they are turned to ministers of sorrow, where shall she look for consolation? Her lot is to be wooed and won; and if unhappy in her love, her heart is like some fortress that has been captured, sacked, abandoned, and left desolate.

How many eyes grow dim, how many soft cheeks grow pale, how many lovely forms fade away into the tomb, and none can tell the cause that blighted their loveliness! As the dove will clasp its wings to its side, and cover and conceal the arrow that is preying on its vitals, so is it the nature of women to hide from the world the pangs of wounded affection. The love of a delicate female is always shy and silent. Even when fortunate, she scarcely breathes it to herself; but when otherwise, she buries it in the recesses of her bosom, and there lets it cower and brood among the ruins of her peace. With her the desire of the heart has failed—the great charm of existence is at an end! She neglects all the cheerful exercises which gladden the spirits, quicken the pulses, and send the tide of life in healthful currents through the veins. Her rest is broken, the sweet refreshment of sleep is poisoned by melancholy dreams, dry sorrow drinks her blood, until her enfeebled frame sinks under the slightest external injury. Look for her after a little while, and you find friendship weeping over her untimely grave, and wondering that one who but lately glowed with all the radiance of health and beauty, should so speedily be brought down to darkness and the worm. You will be told of some wintry chill, some casual indisposition, that laid her low; but no one knows of the mental malady that previously sapped her strength, and made her so easy a prey to the spoiler.

She is like some tender tree, the pride and beauty of the grove—graceful in its form, bright in its foliage, but with the worm preying at its heart. We find it withered when it should be most fresh and luxuriant; we see it drooping its branches to the earth, and shedding leaf by leaf, until, wasted and perished away, it falls even in the stillness of the forest; and as we muse over the beautiful ruin, we strive in vain to recollect the blast or thunderbolt that could have smitten it with decay." This world has many pleasures between the cradle and the grave, yet, alas! how many of them are futile and vain! but the sweetest of them all, and one that will never decay, is to cherish the heart that loves you.

Sermon X

Reviewers

"O that mine enemy had written a book!"

IT was discovered by Dean Swift, and afterwards proven and fully illustrated by Sir Walter Scott, that the patriarch Job was a Reviewer; and it would appear that he had been as malicious and inveterate as any of his successors, when he could think of no better opportunity for exercising his revenge than that his enemy had written a book. What works this ancient and notable Arabian got to review, will always remain a mystery; but we must not suppose that the art of printing was not then discovered, for Job says in one verse, "O that my words were written! O that they were PRINTED in a book!" And as that grand sacred and dramatic poem was translated from the Arabic by Moses while he was herding the flocks of his father-in-law in that country, it would appear, from the superb style of the work, that the literature of Arabia had at that time reached a very high pitch. But in addressing myself to reviewers and readers I must come nearer home; and shall endeavour to lay down some general rules for the art, which ought, in every case, to be attended to, and which never have been attended to as yet.

It is true the occupation of the legitimate reviewer is gone, and has devolved entirely on the editors of newspapers; while the old-established reviews are merely a set of essays, such as these Sermons of mine are.

It is no wonder it should be so, considering the woful want of candour, and miserable political party-spirit, which have pervaded the whole of their lucubrations, from the highest to the lowest; and he who was long accounted the highest, was, in this respect, the worst of them all.

You, then, who handle the rod of literary correction, attend to one who has both been a reviewer and reviewed. Read and judge for yourself; and if told that such and such works are exquisitely fine, and that every one admires them, and that they are composed according to the very best of rules, then suspect a party-spirit, and say not to yourself, of your opponent in politics, "Now has mine enemy written a book." This is so decidedly the case in the present day, that no criticism whatever is the least to be depended on. Why not, like a man of honour and candour, judge of the work solely by the effect it produces on yourself? and then you will rarely be wrong. If the author carries you into the regions of fancy, and amuses you with a creation of new and beautiful images, why not approve of them, though of a different political creed? If he goes along the beaten road of nature, and introduces you to characters having manners and attitudes such as you meet with in the world, why not converse with him as you do with a friend? You ought to give yourself no trouble, whither he goes, or what he does, provided he takes you along with him, and makes an agreeable companion on the road. Never say in your heart, "He is mine enemy who thus delighteth me;" nor ever stoop to be told by another what you are to be pleased with. Your taste and imagination are exclusively your own, and therefore you should be ashamed either to laugh or cry, to abuse or to commend, at the fiat of any save your own taste and judgment.

The exercise of your taste, then, should uniformly be directed to the free and voluntary application of the understanding to the mental food presented to it. Most men will relish what is natural and simple, if they are permitted to judge for themselves. If you take the most admired passages from the best authors, you will find them to be the natural expressions of men of good sense; and you will admire them, because you feel that they are precisely what you would have thought and said yourself on the same occasion; that they are, in fact, the things which have always been thought, but never so well expressed. One generation passeth away, and another generation cometh; but the earth abideth ever, and all races of men admire the same objects. A tree in the full expansion of its branches is beautiful, and a cataract is sublime. The savage as well as the philosopher feels and is delighted with these beauties of nature. Therefore a correct taste, whereby you can judge of the works of others, is nothing more than a common and unprejudiced understanding. Never allow any person to persuade you that criticism is a science, and that an author must go astray unless he follows certain rules. You may just as soon believe that you can acquire the power of distinguishing between bitter and sweet by laying down rules for your palate, as between the low and the sublime by studying the art of poetry.

No rules ever devised by man can make a poet. The fire and rapidity of true genius will always overstep the cold restraints of art; and why should the productions of genius be tied down by the chains and fetters of criticism? The rule ought to be in every man's breast; and if he does not find it there, I would advise him to consider, that perhaps

nature intended him for some more useful profession than that of string-
ing rhymes, or passing sentence on other men's works.

It is the prerogative of genius to take a high and commanding station over the human mind. Were I to give an explanation of the term,
I should call it a power which enables him who possesses it to hold the
greatest number of his fellow-creatures in willing captivity. Its voice
and language address men of different countries and of different ages
with the same effect. Ignorance arises to salute it, and learning bends
to its sway. If it had not been for the ingenious contrivance of men of
profound understandings and cold hearts to fix it down with rules of
their own invention, its power would have been irresistible, and its
dominion extended over the whole world. But perhaps it may be said,
that these rules of the schoolmen of taste are useful for giving us a full
relish of the beauties of fine compositions, and that by teaching us
why and to what extent we should admire, they may improve the
reader, though they are of no benefit to the author; and, if this is admitted, then the said declaimers will tell you, that though it is impossible to form genius by the compasses, the square, and the rule, yet there
are many excrescences in a vivid imagination which the cold hand of
criticism may help to rub away. In this manner those immaculate judges
of matters which should be left to the feelings of mankind, carry on
their usurpations over the powers of the understanding.

Genius may be defined as taste put in motion and displayed; and I
firmly believe, when a man is animated by the fire of nature, and his
mind brought to its full tone of exertion, that he will write more consistently with the rules of common sense, than if fettered by the best
rules that ever reviewer laid down. Besides, the same man whose
thoughts were like lightning while composing his works, may be cool
in revising them. It is not necessary to have one head to invent and
another to censure and correct; for, certainly, the imagination which
sketches the outlines is best qualified to finish the picture. If a man
would do justice to himself, he must hold reviews and reviewers in the
utmost contempt. The original powers of his mind will never be developed, if he cower like a spaniel beneath the lash of the canting critic.
His own taste must be the rule of his composition, else he may be
assured he will be inferior to himself.

There is another advantage which your most sapient arbiters pretend to be of great advantage to the reading public; which is, the point-
ing out to us what ought to be admired, and how and in what manner
we ought to feel the beauties of fine composition, which you seem
quite convinced we could not do without your particular instructions.
We are especially obliged to you for this; for, without doubt, the de-

sign is a charitable one. But if your discrimination is so nice, who pretend to hold the balance of taste in your hands, then, in the first place, you must persuade all men of genius to write directly according to your rules, in order to make this great object of criticism useful and necessary. They must write first to please you, and then you will take care to make their works acceptable and useful to the rest of mankind. The authors are to be the physicians, and you the apothecaries to mix up the dose so as to produce its proper effect.

You may depend on it, almost as much as any article of your faith, that we can never be brought to feel what is beautiful and sublime by the whole art of criticism. Independently of all reasoning, there must be something without us to rouse and carry along, with an irresistible force, some latent principle in our mind. Every man, therefore, should be his own critic, and strive rather to judge for himself than to impose his dogmas on others. I wish particularly to inculcate the advantage of this on a young man beginning to relish and admire the beauties of fine composition,—that he disregard all the absurd rules of reviewers; for he will never obtain a standard for his taste by any precept which another man is pleased to give him; and therefore he will exceedingly increase his labour, if he strive to admire such beauties as are pointed out to him, which he himself did not spontaneously perceive. There are, now-a-days, so many coxcombs of reviewers, that it is most diverting to read their luminous observations. If the author be but of their party in politics, and adhere a little to their dogmatic rules, there is nothing more required; they will point out to you, in perfect raptures, the finest and the most brilliant passages. But if he be of the adverse party, then "their enemy has written a book," and on him they fall tooth and nail. Of all canting in the world, there is none like the canting of criticism. The reviewer looks only at the stop-watch! "Prithee, shepherd, who keeps all these jackasses?" said my uncle Toby.

If we try one of these self-constituted judges with the true touchstone whereby to appreciate genius, we find him generally deficient in taste as well as candour, and that he does not understand the passages he has condemned. It would do our young men of a literary turn of mind much good, if Nature herself were permitted to give the law; and if our reviewers would endeavour rather to write something to be admired, than try to force us to admire what has already been written for some mean or selfish purpose, to serve the interests of a publisher or party. But the plague is, they cannot write any thing to be admired; the greater part of them being a sort of authors discarded by the public as well as the publishers. There are and have been a few splendid exceptions; but taking all the reviewers within the last half century, since reviewing came in fashion, you will find how very few of them were capable of writing a popular original work.

Is it not curious, that it is always in the ruder times of a nation that those works are composed from which critics afterwards derive all their grand rules. There is one period for invention, for the bold creations of an unbridled fancy, and another for the sober decisions of a cool and improved understanding; but the lash of criticism is any thing but favourable to genius. It is an adder in the path, and has marred the mental journey of many an ardent and promising genius, and brought many of them to an untimely grave. If there were such a thing as an impartial critic in the world, which I rather doubt, a bold unprejudiced fellow who would tell his mind freely, fearless of all parties, whether public or private, I would regard him as a treasure to the realm; but the writings of such a man I have never contemplated.

I would, therefore, advise all young men of imagination never to read a work of criticism, ancient or modern; but step back to an early age; and if the original stamina of genius is yours, the fame you covet is secure. Take the simplicity of Moses, the splendour of Job, David, and Isaiah. Take Homer, and, if you like, Hesiod, Pindar, and Ossian; and by all means William Shakespeare. In short, borrow the fire and vigour of an early period of society, when a nation is verging from barbarism into civilisation; and then you will imbibe the force of genius from its original source. Nourish the inspiration, and despise the cold rules of criticism. Even my own school, the traditionary ballads of my country, is better than theirs.

Let nothing, then, persuade any youthful reader, in judging of a composition, to depart from the standard which he has in his own mind. Because you must be certain that there is some defect in the author if his works can please another man before they can please you, or there must be an incurable defect in your taste if every beauty must be pointed out to you before you can perceive or relish it. Despise the idea. Read none of them; but think and judge for yourself. If you had seen the times which I have seen in the Modern Athens, you could not have believed that a certain little great man could have so soon sunk into such utter insignificance.

It is absurd, however, to imagine that our mental relish for the beauties of composition cannot be improved. I am far from advancing an opinion which might encourage either presumption or idleness. But there is a great difference between a bodily frame rendered healthy by exercise, and one whose health depends upon medicine. Therefore, application to good books is of infinitely more use to a young man than to study the comments which have been made on them. There is, also, a refinement in taste, which you will perhaps be fortunate enough to avoid if you never read a work on criticism. This consists in the affectation of feeling beauties which you do not in reality feel, but are merely pinning your faith to another man's sleeve; and a young man is in great danger of falling into the snare, because he thinks his understanding will be called in question, if his admiration does not keep pace with that of the critics. It is only quotations from the latter that are spouted at *soirées*, the main work is never looked into: I have often observed this, and perceived that it was a great evil under the sun.

Prejudice may not always suffer a man to acknowledge it, as it may be his enemy that wrote the book; but I hold it impossible that the exquisite touches of a man of true genius shall fail to excite warmth and admiration in the youthful mind. I adjure you all, then, my young friends, that when you find the inspiration and power of the author carrying you along with him, take a polite leave of the reviewers in as easy a manner as you can. You have learned the mystery of the art, so far as it respects yourself, to much greater advantage than ever you will learn it from them. I believe, too, that every attempt to judge correctly will improve your taste, in the same secret manner in which frequent repetition improves the memory. The only difficulty is, to decide what books you should read; but in this listen to the general voice of mankind, but never to a critic by profession.

I dislike all fine and splendid writing in prose, and admire plain common sense much more; therefore I advise you to give up the study of it, and cultivate that philosophy of the mind which investigates the hidden springs and sources of pleasure in reading; there you will find from the productions of genius pleasures of a purer kind, and at a cheaper rate, than by skimming over the lucubrations of hundreds of reviewers every year. Sit down to your book as you would to conversation; and never harbour an intention of triumph over the defects of your author; but divest yourself of all envy, and read to be pleased, and it is more than probable you will be so. According to the excellency of his work, you will be the more or less pleased; but if he should fail in those particular points which are suited to your fancy, it is an easy matter to take leave of him. But do not get angry and abuse him; you need not act improperly because he writes ill, as you may be sure he did as well as he could. But if you feel pleased with him, that is your own affair; only do not suffer any person, whether friend or reviewer, to tickle you into more delight than you naturally feel. You will enjoy far greater pleasure in discovering the beauties which affect your mind, without being obliged to a prompter. This I consider as the clear gain of taste, which will please you the more as being the fruit of your own industry; and you will likewise discover whether your taste be equal to the genius of your author, and at any rate you will be in the way of making it so.

There is, in fact, a great want of ingenuousness in applying rules which are not your own to the works of others. It is like the honesty of the tailor, who stole a silver foot-rule solely for the purpose of doing justice to his customers. I do not mean merely that you deceive your companions into a better opinion of your taste than it deserves; but candour and fairness in the inner man is honourable and becoming in all men, but especially in the young. Your expressions should not only be the exact copy of your mind, but your very thoughts should be your own, arising naturally from the circumstances that suggest them. Never praise or censure because another person does so, nor pretend to feel because a reviewer or any other pretended to feel before you. There is an amiable candour which sparkles on every benevolent countenance, and there is also a candour which reaches to every thought of the heart; and the one of these is connected with the other. You may think that I am refining too much here, and confounding together the laws of taste with the laws of morality; but really nothing is farther from my meaning. We are so much the beings of habit, that honest ingenuousness in one case secures it in another. Whenever you perceive vanity and affectation in a man, you may view it as a clear proof that the man not only wants understanding, but that his principles are suspicious. Bring, therefore, always an unprejudiced mind to the works of genius, and you will read them with pleasure and improvement. The only rule I have laid down to you all along, and which I again repeat, is, to call no man your master in taste and judgment; and I think you will be able to follow this advice if you find a reviewer pretending to direct your taste, and to discover beauties which were not apparent to you. If the true paintings of nature and character in former ages are not sufficient to form your taste, no law of criticism will ever avail you.

My intention in all this is to persuade you that you have a mental standard, the gift of God, by which you will be able to appreciate the works of genius, and that you will improve that gift by exercise. I deprecate, above all things, an implicit dependence on the opinions of others; but to make some amends for this, I request you to exercise your own judgment as much as possible. The first impressions made on the mind may not always be just; for youthful fancy is too apt to consider the ornament an essential part of the dress, and the gilding often conceals the counterfeit from their eyes, veiling the lack of nerve and sinew. But you may be assured, if you have an original capacity of being pleased with excellence, you will not only soon be able to detect false pretenders to it, but you will soon relish the simple guise of Nature through the modest drapery with which men of true genius always adorn her. Let your judgment alone direct your taste. Be true to yourself, and you will never mistake the painting of a courtesan for the blush of nature and virtue. That this slow and correct exercise of judgment is the right one, may, I think, be proved from the new and additional pleasure we receive from a work of genuine merit every time we peruse it. Perhaps, also, this repeated testimony of an individual, though you are partial to the witness, will lead you as certainly to the best authors as the united testimony of all the reviewers in the world.

Save by translations, I am altogether unacquainted with the exquisite beauties which are to be found in the writings of the ancients; but I have always this consolation, that the translations are better than I could have made them, though I had pored over them one half of my life; so that I think I have some advantages over schoolmen, for I have often corrected the English of some of the best Greek and Latin scholars in Scotland. But in all that regards ancient literature, I am not entitled to say a word. Only be sure always to feel your way; and be sure that you understand your author before you exercise the power of judging. I have been told, indeed, that there is genius in sound, and that a certain combination of words in a foreign language may be so formed as to make the person who hears them giddy or sick, though he do not understand a word of them. This appears to me problematical; and having never seen the experiment made, I can only admire at a distance this vast power of genius over the mind, which converts an artificial combination into a natural sound, intelligible both to man and beasts. This gift, however, must be rare; and I know not where to look for it. I have heard the best parts of Homer read in Greek, and sometimes fancied that I could trace from the tones what he was writing about; but it was all a delusion when it came to be explained. I have heard the lays of Ossian chanted for whole nights and days running, in their original tongue; but then the people could explain nothing, and there my fancy got leave to revel free. I have read, indeed, of navigators who conversed with savages, where both parties made themselves perfectly understood by the other, trafficking together to the utmost minutiæ of price. But the truth is, that if you be not familiar with the language of an author, you are compelled to obtain it by a slow and tedious operation, which I think must often leave disagreeable recollections associated with the finest passages of antiquity.

But, lest I should get beyond my depth on this subject, I shall only add, by way of recapitulation, that there is a pure and unadulterated taste in man which is gratified by the language of nature, and the gratifying of which is similar to our admiration of the beautiful and noble works which are presented to us in the universe. This is the taste with which our mind and judgment are alone connected. It is that relish for nature which genius has the power of painting. But let me remind you of a prostitution of genius, which gives you a representation of nature in the robes of vice, and which tries to please you by an appeal to the passions instead of the judgment. It requires no great talents to adapt this luscious kind of writing to the taste of mankind; but it is always more dangerous in proportion to the genius of the author. Vice steals on the heart when it approaches you under the sanction of wit and talents. The poison is then disguised, and may delight you so much that you may be at a loss to know whether you derive the pleasure from the talents of the author, or from the nature of his descriptions. But let your taste be without ambiguity; relishing what is pure, but avoiding, as you would do a serpent, whatever has a tendency to corrupt your heart; and you may safely regard criticism as a thankless and unprofitable concern, as a great evil under the sun, and the one that has most of all others retarded the development of true and natural genius.

Sermon XI

Deistical Reformers

"The fool hath said in his heart there is no God."

ONE would think there is not so great a fool on earth as to say so in his heart; for my part, I do not believe there is an atheist in the world; else he must be deaf, blind, and insensate. Yet it is worthy of remark, that the term deist is not of older date than the middle of the sixteenth century; the class of unbelievers who now assume this appellation were till then denominated atheists; and it was to avoid the odium of that name that they arrogated to themselves the less forbidding and alarming title by which they are now distinguished. Now, as I look upon unbelief as the leading sin of the age, I regard it my duty to contribute my mite towards the preservation of the sublime truths of Christianity, fully convinced of the pernicious effects of infidelity on the virtue and happiness of mankind, and the guilt and danger in which it involves all who embrace it for a rejection of Christianity, as it certainly leads to speculative and practical atheism, as the sparks fly upward.

What is that thing called natural religion which the deist clings to? for I declare I do not comprehend it. Has it a local habitation and a name in any nation under heaven, or is it merely a theory for speculating upon? Does it promise its adherents either peace, safety, or future happiness? Christianity has a footing in the world, and is still gaining ground, but where is this cherished religion of the deist to be found? If it were the religion of nature, how comes it that the God of nature has extinguished it from the face of the earth, save from the mouths of captious cavillers? It is only to be found in the alleged capacity of certain men to discover it, or in the mouths and writings of those who are obliged to borrow its doctrines from holy writ.

The history of mankind is like the history of an individual. There is one period in which the mind is open to impressions, and credulous even to folly; and there is another in which philosophy attempts to combat truth. Our country is, I think, fast approaching to this last stage of existence. Our very priests, who, in the opinion of the modern class of infidels have so long triumphed over the human understanding, now admit that it was the failing of mankind, a few centuries ago, to believe in every absurdity which their predecessors in their ignorance imposed on them. The error of this age is to believe too little, save in some things more extravagantly ridiculous than was ever promulgated in any former age. But if we go on improving at the present rate, I should not be surprised to see a set of philosophers endeavouring to persuade the world to believe in nothing, not even in Rowism itself.

Wisdom, I apprehend, consists in knowing both what to receive and what to reject; and I have made up my mind that no ridicule which a deist can throw on the religion of Jesus shall ever eradicate from my belief one item of the truth of that Divine institution; and if my simple and humble efforts can establish but one wavering soul in the same resolution, I shall consider my time well bestowed. I deem it more contemptible to be a deist than the slave of superstition. Ridicule is the instrument of their persecution; and as they stop at no manner of blasphemy, I have often found it difficult to contain my countenance, and refrain from tears, at hearing the profligacy of the sentiments of learned men. But as the terror of death should never make me a bigot, neither can all the arguments of philosophy or force of ridicule I have ever heard convert me to deism.

Because, let us consider what deism leaves us for what it deprives us of. Christianity has a tendency to make us morally good; it provides us with a simple and complete rule of duty, which no scheme of philosophy has ever been able to accomplish; it has furnished us with motives to the cultivation of holiness the most suitable and persuasive that can possibly be conceived; it addresses itself to all the powers and susceptibilities of our nature; it operates through the decisions of the understanding and through the affections of the heart; it speaks to our love, to our hope and our fear, to our gratitude and our interest; and in the arguments by which it works upon us there is a grandeur, an authority, and a pathos, which I should think no contemplative mind could resist. It tells us we are placed under the government of that Great Being who created and sustains the universe; it unfolds to our view a scene of future retribution the most awful and impressive which imagination can paint, whose throne is to be occupied by Jehovah, whose transactions are to embrace the character and fate of every individual of our race, and whose awards are those of immutable rectitude, and stretch into the boundless duration of eternity; and through life it represents us as constantly under the eye of our Maker, which never leaves us for a moment on the path of life. It tells us that He is present with us at all times and in all places, directing us in every step, fortifying us against every temptation, administering to our aid when we trust in him and require it, putting a proper check on every evil propensity, and presenting a suitable stimulus to every generous, kind, and amiable affection. In short, that our Saviour shall be our God and our guide unto death, and through death and after death our exceeding rich rewarder.

What does poor, cold, forlorn infidelity leave us for all this? No more than to wring our bosoms with the most poignant distress and despair, at the very moment when we stand most in need of consolation. It tells us that when we consign our nearest and dearest friends to the mercy of a Redeemer, that we indulge in a foolish delusion; that they have no tie, no hold of a Mediator; that all the prayers we put up for them are vain, and vain every hope that we cherish for them. "I would rather be a dog and bay the moon," than brow the heaven, and to God's own face deny the revelation of his will to man.

Away with such cold-hearted and gloomy speculations! They shed a misery over the human heart which no sophistry can dissipate. In the day of distress their comforts can sound like nothing but mockery and scorn. They bid us renounce our Saviour, and banish that Comforter who cherished and upheld us; and then where can we go, or where turn ourselves, or where else seek for the words of eternal life?

But let us reason the matter without enthusiasm or violence. Is it not more wise and honourable, then, to refrain from adopting opinions of any apparent danger, till we have considered them in all their bearings and consequences? On the one hand I dare not enter deeply into the mysteries of revelation, nor into the ingenious speculations of the freethinkers on the other. But one of the great objections of the latter to the doctrines of Christianity and the Trinity is, its being so involved in mystery as to be incomprehensible; therefore, they take it upon them to laugh at it and hold it up to ridicule. But, O fools that they are and slow of heart! do they not plainly see that wherever there is a display of the power or wisdom of God, either in revelation or the kingdom of nature, there also they will find a mystery beyond the capacity of human reason to unfold? On this incomprehensible ground, then, I shall never encounter the advocates of unbelief in the doctrines of the Gospel, because they could never know when I was right, and I should always be sure that they were wrong. There is no kind of wit so easy as that which tends to ridicule what neither you nor your adversary can possibly understand. I think it is therefore best, in supporting the doctrines of the Christian religion, always to avoid any attempt to explain mysteries. The necessity and belief of a mystery is one thing, but the explanation another.

Let us never, therefore, even when we ponder on questions in which our eternal interests may be connected, try to involve them in the darkness of philosophical investigation, because a speculative mind may take the wrong side on the clearest subject; and supposing a revelation from God to be necessary, what kind of revelation would it be if it were composed with the intention of solving all the doubts of scepticism?

There is one thing in which we have greatly the advantage over the deist: our professions are all the same in every material point relating to the doctrine of grace and salvation. Every one of them whom I have either heard preach or reason, differs from another, and generally from all the rest. Let us take all the arguments of those who are endeavouring to mislead our minds, and we shall find that there are not two of the whole number who agree in the material points which they wish to establish, while they entirely agree as to those truths of religion which they wish to destroy. They have arrived at a degree of knowledge and illumination at which they are able to perceive all the pretended absurdities of Christianity; but they have not yet reached that sublimity of exaltation which enables them to give something equally useful and interesting as a substitute. Keep always this in view when you begin to study the quibbles of the men who would mislead your minds from the sacred and sublime truths of Christianity, and ask your hearts what do they leave you in its place.

You will then perceive, that in every thing relating either to religion or morality, that that man is not an apostle who pretends merely to pull down; it is also necessary that he be able to build up. If he only does the one without the other, he shews you that he has the power of darkening truth, of suggesting doubts, and disturbing the peace of your mind, without satisfying the longing soul as to any better mode of attaining present or future felicity. His mind is ingenious to mislead, but not candid to impart the knowledge you desire. A man of ordinary ingenuity is able to involve the plainest dictates of reason in obscurity and darkness; and much more may he gain an imaginary triumph over many of the truths of revelation, which from their very nature we are incapable of explaining. But I stand by this, and it is an argument I shall repeat to the end, that it is no objection to a truth revealed as essentially necessary to our comfort, that it is above our comprehension. This is one of the deist's great bulwarks; but my view of it is, that it is nothing more than employing the reason which God has bestowed upon us to defeat the benevolent purposes of his gift.

I would ask the sceptic if he does not observe any traces of wisdom or intelligence in the works of nature? if there is no specific revelation of the unity and power of the Godhead in the Scriptures? or, in short, if there is any thing in the world which he receives as a truth which he cannot comprehend? If he answers in the affirmative, as he must, then where is his great bulwark? His objection is levelled not against the truths of revelation alone, but against the possibility of conveying truths of any kind to the mind of man; and whoever persists in it, it will infallibly lead to gross ignorance or obstinate atheism. We enjoy the blessings of sense in this sublunary state without the assistance of philosophy, and when we reason on the sources of pleasure and the causes of our enjoyment, we bewilder ourselves in uncertain conjectures, yet we still continue to enjoy. I wish to God that we were able in the same manner to taste the sweets of Divine truth, while we are vainly endeavouring to comprehend it: but in this glorious mental feast to doubt is to destroy the relish.

The truths of revelation were never intended to satisfy the doubts of philosophical infidelity. Those parts of them which give us information concerning the purity and perfections of God can never be subjected to the decisions of man; and those which relate to our duty were never intended for the disquisitions of captious philosophers. The first, from their own nature, require us to exercise humility; and the second are so plain, that any man who does not attempt to reason on them must understand them. Suppose, for an instant, that Divine revelation were every thing which the wisest of mankind could make it, would that, do you think, secure it from the carpings of vain philosophy? Is it to be at all supposed that their pride and their desire of distinction who at present oppose those truths would not find something to alter or improve? Believe it not; for there are always such a number of restless, discontented beings in the world, that there is no established or happy system which they will not attack. But believe this, that their objections to the Christian religion which affect your mind are the offspring of weakness or passion, not of reason. I will venture to assert, that there is no truth, human or Divine, which interested, selfish, and ingenious men, will not try to combat. It is of no consequence how forcibly or clearly the truth is stated, as neither its intrinsic value, the evidence by which it is supported, nor the common sense of mankind, can defend it from attack; and if this assertion be admitted, we need not be surprised that Christianity has in every age been opposed by the whole force of human wisdom. There are no truths in it flattering to the present state of man, nor is it safe to tell the sceptical philosopher that he is a poor, weak-minded, short-sighted mortal—that his wisdom is folly, and his pretensions ridiculous; and that if he finds himself possessed of a fund of reason and a power of mind capable of resisting the plainest dictates of revelation, how is it possible to teach him humility? I beseech you, therefore, before you come to any determination concerning the truths of religion, to consider whether they be adapted to the state of man, or merely to the minds of philosophers. Provided they instruct the ignorant, and are calculated to give peace and comfort to the numerous classes of mankind, to restrain vice and give the assurances of pardon and a future life to the miserable and the guilty and to those who are ready to perish, then why should we abandon them though a few ingenious and cool-minded men should endeavour to persuade us that they are unnecessary? If it is true on the one hand that no system of truth could be adapted to all the peculiarities of their minds, it is equally true on the other that all their reasoning against revelation is founded on conjecture, and, from the very nature of the subject, can never be conclusive.

In the history of mankind it would appear, that there have been all along a certain proportion of them created with dispositions to oppose all established rules and rights; and this disposition is still gaining ground, threatening to overthrow both churches and states. I am sorry to observe, that among a numerous class of wretched politicians every one of them is tinctured with the principles of infidelity. I should not have said every one of them, for I hope in God there are some exceptions; but I solemnly declare, that as far as I am acquainted with their writings and characters, they are all grovelling in the mire of scepticism, and not only so, but exulting in their high attainment in this, resembling their great archetype. Although it will look very odd in the middle of a sermon, and a serious, well-meant one too, I cannot help inserting here a few lines from a certain Ode to the Devil, once quoted by a brilliant northern maiden, now labouring under a hopeless consumption:—

> Hail patriot spirit! thy labours be ——;
> For of all great Reformers thyself wert the first:
> Thou wert the first with discernment strong,
> To perceive that all rights divine were wrong;
> And long hast thou spent thy sovereign breath,
> In heaven above and in earth beneath,
> And roused it from thy burning throne,
> The glory of independence alone;
> Proclaiming to all, with fervour and irony,
> That kingly dominion's all humbug and tyranny,
> And whoso listeth may be free;
> For freedom, full freedom, 's the word with thee;

That life has its pleasures, the rest is a sham,
And all that comes after a flim and a flam.

This doctrine of our arch enemy's is the prevailing one among our grand reforming sceptics of the present day; but surely these men never examine both sides of the question, else there are some leading truths which would carry conviction with them. They would see that God is the wise and just governor of the world; that he is merciful, and man unworthy. These truths, if at all considered, are adapted to the level of every man's capacity and conscience; and therefore the only objection to them must be the particular form which they assume in the Scriptures. Admitting that God is just and merciful, and that man is guilty, yet our reforming philosophers are not satisfied with the peculiar manner of God's exercising that justice and mercy, nor yet with the terms on which future life is offered to them. If the doctrines are supported by the interpositions of the Deity, they deny the facts; and if we employ reasoning, they reject our conclusions. What, then, is to be done with men possessed of this subtile and wonderful power of denying every thing? In my humble opinion, we should just allow them to doubt and cavil on until they give us something in place of Christianity on which they wish us to depend, and then we may acquire the art of doubting in as great perfection as themselves. There is nothing in the compass of nature, or in the possibility of revealed truth, of which either a weak or ingenious man may not bring himself to doubt. Confusion, or acuteness of mind, may equally lead to the possession of this happy talent. The doctrines of revelation are indefinite with respect to our reason. If we could have discovered them of ourselves they would not have been revealed; and therefore it is better and safer for us to lay hold of what is offered, than to doubt because we cannot comprehend.

It is a singular fact, that those men who pretend to believe in nothing revealed to them, are yet as fond of accounting for some favourite dogmas of their own as if they were in full possession of a reasonable faith. The power of doubting seems only to extend to received opinions; as if the human mind had not yet arrived at that intuitive perfection which makes the rejection of a truth tantamount to the establishment of a system. This fortunately brings our reforming philosophers to the level of other men, and gives us the privilege of examining the articles of their faith, before we are bewildered by their speculations. It is best for us, then, always in our disputes and conversations with them to bring the matter to this decisive point. The truth may suffer in our hands from their superior acuteness, and we may be unable to penetrate into their motives for misleading us, but in a point so material as the subversion of our faith respecting doctrines on which we have been accustomed to rest our salvation, it will be wise for us, in the first instance, to hear what truths they have agreed to substitute in place of those which they are persuading us to relinquish. This simple method of preserving and defending ourselves I have recommended from the beginning, and do so once more; and you will find that it will puzzle our reforming philosophical friends much more than the finest reasoning.

We come into the field on unequal terms with men who have already lost the best stake of their hopes and happiness. Let us make them bring, therefore, the little which they can promise into competition with the immense sums we are to lose; and if they can afford us no equivalent, why should we listen to them? and if they cannot agree among themselves, it is best to leave them alone till they do so. Some of them pretend, by the force of human reason alone, to give us more exalted views of the nature and perfections of God than those which we receive from the Sacred Oracles. But on the supposition that their claims equal their presumption, we have still to inquire from what sources they derived their information, and in what manner their superior discoveries have influenced their conduct to the God whom they worship. The first of these inquiries leads us back to the times when the revelation of God did not illumine the darkness of nature, or to the places into which its beams have not yet penetrated; and the second, to the men with whom we have to contend—these grand reformers of all existing things.

On looking back to the former ages of the world, we find certain periods in their history in which mankind were as far advanced in civilisation and the arts of life as we are, yet in which they were far behind us in every thing respecting the truths of religion, and the knowledge either of the unity or the perfections of God. It is held as a kind of literary profanation to entertain any doubts of the learning, taste, or wisdom of the ancients. It is true, indeed, that in the greater part of their writings which have been transmitted, they discover a knowledge of human nature, a genuine simplicity and a power of mind, which have not yet been equalled in modern productions. But on all subjects connected with religion or a future state, their opinions are held in little estimation even by the deistical reformers of our religion themselves. But these very men, who deny the truth of Divine revelation, have acquired notions concerning many of its doctrines which the wisest and best men of antiquity could never discover. They admit them into their creed, while they deny the source whence they derived them. I will not say it is want of candour, but it must either be that or want of attention which leads them into this absurdity; and it behoves us not only to use the light of revelation, as they have done, as the means of purifying our notions, but to let it guide us through the intricacies with which our minds are entangled, and bring us onward to immortal life. Why should we be indebted to the word of God for the sole purpose of enlarging our minds, and not receive from it the important benefits which it may confer? We should laugh at a philosopher who denied the existence of the sun, while it was the occupation of his life to collect his beams into a bottle, or separate them by a prism.

It is useful, also, for us to observe the improvement which those who deny the Scriptures have derived from the discoveries of the Divine Nature, which they pretend to have made by the new and extraordinary exertions of human reason; but let us follow the simple rule of Scripture, and judge of opinions by their fruits. I hope we need no reasoning to convince us that in proportion as we are acquainted with the works and perfections of God, we shall be the more disposed to mingle reverence with our worship, and to cherish humility in our hearts. Independently of Divine revelation, these are dispositions necessarily stamped on the nature and condition of man. Were the most obstinate unbeliever permitted to behold the majesty and splendour of Divine power in a more direct and comprehensive manner than he is able to trace it in its effects, we may rest satisfied that his feelings would correspond with his situation. The professed intention of the Holy Scriptures is to produce this desirable effect on the minds of those who believe in them. Some may object to the truths revealed, but no reasonable man can ever object to the adoration and humility which they are fitted to excite. They have not only given us very exalted views of God who created and governs the world, but of the imbecility of any of his creatures to contend with him or dispute his power and omnipotence, after looking abroad upon the heavens and the earth. How beautifully sublime are some of the expressions of the sacred volume relating to this!

Where wast thou when I laid the foundations of the earth? declare, if thou hast understanding. Who hath laid the measures thereof, if thou knowest? or who hath stretched the line upon it? Whereupon are the foundations thereof fastened? or who laid the corner-stone thereof when the morning-stars sang together, and all the sons of God shouted for joy? Or who shut up the sea with doors when it brake forth as if it had issued out of the womb? when I made the cloud the garment thereof, and a thick swaddling band for it, and brake up for it my decreed place, and set bars and doors, and said, Hitherto shalt thou come, but no further; and here shall thy proud waves be stayed?

Hell is naked before him, and destruction hath no covering. He stretcheth forth the north over the empty place, and hangeth the earth upon nothing. He bindeth up the waters in his thick clouds; and the cloud is not rent under them. He holdeth back the face of his throne, and spreadeth his cloud upon it. He hath compassed the waters with bounds, until the day and night come to an end. The pillars of heaven tremble and are astonished at his reproof. He divideth the sea with his power, and by his understanding he smiteth through the proud. By his spirit he hath garnished the heavens; his hand hath formed the crooked serpent. Lo, these are parts of his ways; but how little a portion is heard of him? but the thunder of his power who can understand?

He bowed the heavens, and came down; and darkness was under his feet. And he rode upon a cherub, and did fly; yea, he did fly upon the wings of the wind. He made darkness his secret place: his pavilion round about him were dark waters and thick clouds of the skies. At the brightness that was before him his thick clouds passed; hailstones and coals of fire. The Lord also thundered in the heavens, and the Highest gave his voice; hailstones and coals of fire. Yea, he sent out his arrows and scattered them; he shot out lightnings, and discomfited them. Then the channels of the waters were seen, and the foundations of the world were discovered at thy rebuke, O Lord! at the blast of the breath of thy nostrils.

When I consider thy heavens, the work of thy fingers; the moon and the stars, which thou hast ordained; what is man that thou art mindful of him, and the son of man, that thou visitest him! O Lord our Lord, how excellent is thy name in all the earth!

The heavens declare the glory of God; and the firmament sheweth his handywork. Day unto day uttereth speech, night unto night sheweth knowledge. There is no speech nor language where their voice is not heard. Their line is gone through all the earth, and their words to the end of the world. In them hath he set a tabernacle for the sun; which is as a bridegroom coming out of his chamber, and rejoiceth as a strong man to run his race.

I could multiply a hundred more, all tending to prove that those men to whom the promises of eternal life were very dark and uncertain, and the way of salvation through a Redeemer totally unknown; for the prophecies of him being the words of inspiration, the men knew not with any distinctness what they were prophesying about; but all of them perceived the hand of an Almighty Creator and Governor of the universe, by looking abroad on the face of nature, and acknowledged him in these magnificent exulting strains. And, moreover, the characters of the sacred writers, and of all those whom they describe as the servants of God, give many plain and perspicuous proofs of the power and influence of the truths of revelation, especially in their worship.

Is it not, therefore, to be expected that our modern deists, who have made discoveries of the Divine nature far more exalted and sublime, should surpass all other men in the regularity and fervour of their devotions? We need not expect that they should be enthusiasts, because philosophy has waged eternal war against imagination; but surely they should give us the form or the example of a pure and spiritual worship, suitable to the pretended dignity of their own minds, and more calculated to express the feelings and wants of a reasonable nature, than any thing we have been able to derive from the word of God.

Now, really what is the character of the grand reformers of our religion, morals, and government? This is one of the grounds whereon to try those who believe in the Scriptures, and those who do not: and with all the attention which I have been able to give to the subject, I have found the latter greatly deficient in that adoration and gratitude which we all owe to our Creator and Preserver. I have conversed with many of them for the last twenty-six years, listened to all their reasoning without daring to interfere with my rude and vulgar speech; and of late I have looked into their writings, both philosophical and moral, as far as it lay in my power in the wilderness, and I do not find that their exalted notions of the Godhead have once suggested the necessity of worship at all. I have attended minutely to their whole conduct, and I have no reason to believe that they are guilty of frequent or fervent prayer to God. If ever they are caught in the act, we cannot fail to observe that it is only under severe affliction, when their minds are softened and annealed, or when the prospect of death had fairly overcome the principles of their philosophy.

I speak not here of the delightful employment of giving up the mind and spirit to our heavenly Father, of the soothing consolation of depending on superior strength, or of the rapturous joy of a grateful heart; but I maintain that the worship of God by direct adoration, by reverence, or by devout meditation on his power, goodness, and compassion, is the natural result of our acquaintance with these Divine perfections; and that if our reforming deists do not worship in sincerity as their Christian brethren do, what can we think but that their pretended knowledge is affectation, love of singularity, and pride of heart, and that they are in the gall of bitterness and bond of iniquity?

If, on the other hand, the researches of our friends are leading them to absolute scepticism, I think we have as good reason to doubt of their understanding as they have to doubt of our faith. I can perceive no advantage to be gained from a creed which has no fixed principles. It gives the mind no solid ground of confidence for the present, and deprives it of all hope for the future. We should surely rather take our chance of going wrong, than the certainty of having nothing; for if a man doubts of the principles of his religion, of truths which other men believe to be established, of the existence of God, of the immortality of the soul, and of a future state, he may be in equal doubt whether any of his own speculations are well founded, and therefore his unbelief carries along with it a reason for its condemnation.

To sum up, then: O, my friends, beware how you desert the sunny braes of the gospel of Jesus, for the cold barren wastes of infidelity. What does the latter present to us but a total negation of all which tends most effectually to cheer us under the calamities of our lot in this life, presenting us with a dreary path in which there is neither a shadow from the heat, nor a shelter from the storm, of Divine wrath. And what a vista of eternity! A shoreless sea without star or beacon, or hope of heaven for evermore. But, clinging to the mild and heavenly doctrines of Christianity, we partake of the blessings of this life with a far purer and higher relish, when we regard them as bestowed by the hand of an all-perfect God, and when we receive them through the channel of a mercy secured to us by the mediation of his own Son, and when we contemplate them as pledges and hostages of better things to come. But such is the effect of deism, that it withers the charm of every earthly blessing, reducing it to the mere level of a degraded animal gratification, and leaves us to feed upon it like the beasts that perish, without a thought that rises above the dust or that points beyond the grave. Where then is the balm which we may apply with effect to our wounded hearts in the days of trouble and adversity, when we have rejected the aid of our Almighty Physician? But though all the troubles of life overtake us, give us but the privilege with contrite hearts to cast ourselves below the cross of our Redeemer, and pillow our heads on the bosom of Omnipotence, and we shall rise superior to all affliction, and rejoice in tribulation.

Let us think also of the value of our immortal souls before we give up that great bond of a Mediator between God and man. The sun, the moon, and stars, shall pass away; and as a vesture shall they be changed, having served their purposes; but the soul shall endure; and after they shall all have been blotted out from the wide expanse of universal nature, the soul shall still survive, and stretch out its existence into everlasting ages, and spend that eternity to which it is destined, either under the burden and anguish of a just condemnation, or in the enjoyment of exalted, unmingled, and never-ending bliss. Then think what must be the doom of that soul which casts off its allegiance to God, and bids an infidel defiance to the revelation of his will and his glorious scheme of redemption.

THE END.

Note on the Text

Although it was in general well received on its first appearance in 1834, *A Series of Lay Sermons* did not run to a second edition. Furthermore, this book was omitted from all the various nineteenth-century collected editions of Hogg's writings. As a result, more than a hundred and sixty years were to pass between the first publication of *A Series of Lay Sermons* and its second publication, an event which took place with the appearance of the present volume of the Stirling / South Carolina edition of James Hogg.

Nineteenth-century texts can exist in a great variety of early versions: for example, the author's manuscript might survive, as might proofs of the first edition; and the first edition might have been followed by a sequence of subsequent editions, each introducing a new crop of variant readings. The editor of *A Series of Lay Sermons* is faced with no such complexity. Hogg's manuscript does not survive, nor do proofs; and there were no nineteenth-century reprintings. In these circumstances, the present edition is necessarily a reprint of the only extant previous version of the text, the first edition of 1834. A few emendations have been made, to correct what appear to be errors by the printer in the first edition; but otherwise the present edition seeks to follow the first edition exactly. These emendations may be listed as follows. The page number is given for each item in the list, with the line number following. In calculating line numbers, titles and running headlines have been ignored.

33, l.13 almost intolerable] almost intolerant (*first edition*)
34, l.32 rational solidity.] national solidity (*first edition*)
40, l.2 to another?"] to another? (*first edition*)
54, ll.18-19 but meantime the] but me antime the (*first edition*)
56, l.37 are the business] are the busines (*first edition*)
57, l.10 *thou not.*] *thou not* (*first edition*)
67, l.7 have before us a] have before a (*first edition*)
78, l.16 These disquisitions are so] The disputes are so (*first edition*: 'disputes' here may have been caused by eye-slip from the 'disputes' that follows a few words later)
79, l.23 the best chance] the least chance (*first edition*)
82, ll.5-6 from our friends,] from our friend, (*first edition*)
98, ll.21-22 with decay."] with decay. (*first edition*)

113, l.10 adapted to all] adopted to all (*first edition*)
119, 1.5 chance of going] choice of going (*first edition*)
119, 1.26 leaves us to feed] leaves to feed (*first edition*)

End-of-line hyphens in the first edition of *A Series of Lay Sermons* are ignored in the present edition, except in cases in which it seems likely that the word in question would have been given a hyphen even if it had not appeared at the end of a line: in most instances guidance has been obtained from appearances of the word in question elsewhere in the text.

Various words are hyphenated at the ends of lines in the present edition of *A Series of Lay Sermons*. The list below indicates those cases in which such hyphens should be retained in quotation.

16, l. 1 stretched-forth   35, l.34 never-ending
16, l. 8 crisping-pins   63, l.25 deplorable-looking
23, l.12 well-being   78, l. 4 well-bred
30, l.12 good-nature   85, l.35 all-wise

Douglas S. Mack

Notes

In the Notes which follow, page references include a letter enclosed in brackets: (a) indicates that the passage concerned is to be found in the first quarter of the page, while (b) refers to the second quarter, (c) to the third quarter, and (d) to the fourth quarter. The Bible is referred to in the Authorised King James version that would have been familiar to Hogg and his contemporaries. It is clear that Hogg frequently quotes from the Bible from memory, and is therefore sometimes inexact: these instances are indicated by the word 'see' preceding the reference. For references to plays by Shakespeare the edition used has been *The Complete Works: Compact Edition*, ed. by Stanley Wells and Gary Taylor (Oxford: Clarendon Press, 1988). The Notes are greatly indebted to standard works such as the *Dictionary of National Biography* and the *Oxford English Dictionary*. Other works extensively used in the Notes are referred to by the following abbreviations:

Memoir or *Familiar Anecdotes*   James Hogg, *Memoir of the Author's Life* and *Familiar Anecdotes of Sir Walter Scott*, ed. by Douglas S. Mack (Edinburgh and London: Scottish Academic Press, 1972)

Garden   Mrs. Garden, *Memorials of James Hogg, the Ettrick Shepherd* (Paisley and London, [n.d.])

Parr   Norah Parr, *James Hogg at Home: Being the Domestic Life and Letters of the Ettrick Shepherd* (Dollar: Douglas S. Mack, 1980)

Dedication

Dr. William Dunlop William Dunlop (1792-1848) studied medicine at Glasgow and became an army doctor, going to Canada in 1813 and India in 1817. In India he edited various newspapers and was an active promotor of a scheme to colonise the island of Saugar, which was infested with tigers—this and his shock of red hair gave him his nickname of 'Tiger' Dunlop. He returned to Scotland in May 1820 after his health broke down and set up practice in Edinburgh, occupying himself with journalism while waiting for patients to arrive, and giving a course of lectures on medical jurisprudence. During this period he published several articles in *Blackwood's Edinburgh Magazine* signed 'Colin Bannantyne', including a letter, 'To the Ettrick Shepherd' (volume 16, July 1824, pp.86-90), a comical review of a French book 'on the art of beautifying one's self' (p.86), which Dunlop adapted to the supposed manners of the Borders, mocking both the book's author and Hogg himself. Hogg presumably became acquainted with Dunlop during these Edinburgh years. In the summer of 1826 Dunlop sailed to Canada to assist John Galt, was appointed Warden of the Forests to the Canada Company, and helped to found the town of Guelph. In the early 1830s he became, like Hogg himself, associated with *Fraser's Magazine*, where he appears in the collective portrait of the magazine's contributors facing 'The Fraserians', *Fraser's Magazine*, 11 (January 1835), 1-27. He was in England between 1831 and 1833, and presumably renewed his friendship with Hogg during the latter's London visit during the first quarter of 1832. Dunlop was an extremely sociable man, and famous for brewing punch. He returned to Canada and died there on 29 June 1848. For further information, see J. G. Dunlop, *The Dunlops of Dunlop: and of Auchenskaith, Keppoch, and Gairbraid* (Frome and London, 1939).

Preface

3(a) an old French monk this putative author is similar to 'old Isaac the curate' in *The Three Perils of Man*, ed. by Douglas Gifford (Edinburgh and London: Scottish Academic Press, 1972), passim.

3(b) In 1801 the year in which Hogg's first publication *Scottish Pastorals* came out; they are perhaps alluded to here as 'a MS. volume of songs, ballads, &c.'.

Sermon I. Good Principles

text an adaptation of Jacob's exclamation in Genesis 42.38.

6(b) evening of life a commonplace derived from Psalm 90.5-6.

6(b) if he passes forty-five Hogg had married in 1820 at the age of forty-nine. His bride, Margaret Phillips, was twenty years younger than her husband. Hogg and his wife had five children, four daughters and a son.

6(d) If he is poor, he is neglected a commonplace incitement to matrimony in the essay-periodical tradition, which Hogg had employed earlier in 'Misery of an Old Batchelor', *The Spy*, No.16 (15 December 1810), pp.120-27 (pp.120-21).

6(d) rising up [...] to bless him possibly an echo of Proverbs 31.28, although this refers to the response of children to a virtuous mother rather than a father.

7(c) their worthy pastor as Hogg is speaking of his neighbours at Altrive, the pastor here would probably be Dr Robert Russell, the incumbent of Yarrow from September 1791 until his death in March 1847. Born in 1766, Russell was married in 1803 to Agnes Turnbull, and had three children. His daughter Agnes (born in 1804) married George Ballantyne, the farmer of Whitehope, while his elder son James (born in 1809) succeeded him as minister to the parish—see Hew Scott, *Fasti Ecclesiae Scoticanae*, 9 vols (Edinburgh, 1915-61), II (1917), 197-98. A family friendship was clearly maintained between the Hoggs and the Russells—see James Russell, *Reminiscences of Yarrow* (Selkirk, 1894), p.139 and passim.

7(d) asserting, with Voltaire no such passage in the writings of Voltaire (François Marie Arouet, 1694-1778) has been traced. Although Voltaire was notoriously not a Christian and held no belief in the immortality of the soul it seems an unlikely statement from him: firstly, because it might be supposed that such a voluminous writer would have hoped for some sort of immortality through his written works, and secondly because he had no children.

8(d) Mr. James Russell James Russell was the minister of Yarrow's son, born on 1 December 1809. In a reference Hogg wrote for him on 7 December 1833 he said, 'I have known Mr. James Russell intimately from his boyhood [...] I esteem him very highly as an associate, a gentleman, and a sound and elegant preacher of the gospel of Jesus'—see Garden, p.331. He acted as his father's assistant in the parish from 1831 onwards, and in July 1841 was ordained his assistant and successor—see Hew Scott, *Fasti Ecclesiae Scoticanae*, 9 vols (Edinburgh, 1915-61), II (1917), 198.

8(d) otium cum dignitate a common Latin expression meaning 'leisure with dignity'; retirement after a person has worked and saved enough to live upon with comfort.

8(d) my younger competitors Hogg expressed similar sentiments in a letter to Robert Gilfillan of 25 January 1834: 'As this is the 64th anniversary of my birth, you need not expect much more from the old Shepherd. Yet I feel my head as clear as ever, although the enthusiasm of love and poetry is sorely abated. I, however, have a good and sterling assistant and successor in you'—see Garden, p.315.

9(d) dark and silent mansions of the grave George Crabbe, *The Library*, line 106, 'the lasting mansions of the dead'.

10(c) our single talent a reference to the parable of the talents (Matthew 25.14-30). A master going on a journey gives five talents (a substantial sum of money) to one servant, two talents to another, and a single talent to a third. The first two servants put their talents to good use, making them increase. This wins them praise when the master returns; but the third servant is condemned, because he has hidden his single talent away, and has not made it increase.

11(a) under the sun a phrase frequently used in Ecclesiastes, for example at 8.15: 'a man hath no better thing under the sun than to eat, and to drink, and to be merry: for that shall abide with him of his labour the days of his life, which God giveth him under the sun'.

11(a) hand findeth to do from Ecclesiastes 9.10: 'Whatsoever thy hand findeth to do, do it with thy might; for there is no work, nor device, nor knowledge, nor wisdom, in the grave, whither thou goest'.

11(a) the last bourn death is 'the undiscovered country from whose bourn/ No traveller returns' in *Hamlet*, III.1.81-82.

11(a) knowledge nor device continuing the allusion to Ecclesiastes 9.10, quoted in the note to 11(a) above.

11(d) apothegms terse sayings, giving an important truth in few words.

12(a) cannie lucky, of good omen.

12(a) "Let no such man be trusted" see Shakespeare's *The Merchant of Venice*, V.1.88.

14(a) wear off guard against, repel.

14(d) man of the mountains a mountain-man is one of the persecuted Covenanters of the seventeenth century: Hogg is alluding to his origins in the mountainous Borders, and to his present role of sermon-giver.

14(d) "Tongues in trees, [...] every thing." from Shakespeare's *As You Like It*, II.1.16-17.

14(d) a dear and esteemed friend John Wilson (1785-1854) had been appointed Professor of Moral Philosophy at the University of Edinburgh in 1820, despite having no qualifications for the post. Hogg first met Wilson after the publication of Wilson's poem *The Isle of Palms* in 1812 and the friendship was maintained with few interruptions until Hogg's death in 1835. Wilson's other long poem *The City of the Plague* (1816), was succeeded by several prose fictions, including *Lights and Shadows of Scottish Life* (1822), to which Hogg's own *The Three Perils of Woman* (1823) was in part a response; *The Trials of Margaret Lyndsay* (1823); and *The Foresters* (1825). Wilson, however, was better known for his authorship of many of the 'Noctes Ambrosianæ' of *Blackwood's Edinburgh Magazine*, in which he featured as the magazine's editor, 'Christopher North'. Hogg was caricatured in the series as the Shepherd, a rustic genius of uncouth manners, a portrait which gave great offence to his wife and at times even to himself, and also misrepresented him to the general reading public of the day.

15(a) fondness foolish affection; want of judgement.

Sermon II. Young Women

text see Isaiah 3.16, 18-23: *cauls* are nets for the hair or close-fitting women's caps; *tires* are ornaments for a woman's head-dress; *tablets* are flat ornaments of precious metal or of a jewel worn on the person; *crisping-pins* are instruments for curling the hair.

16(b) our evangelical prophet's although the prophet Isaiah lived in old testament times, and could not therefore literally hold that salvation is by faith in the atoning death of Christ, he is frequently referred to as 'the evangelical prophet' because so many passages in the book of Isaiah seem to describe the person, sufferings, and redemptive role of Jesus.

16(c) Isaiah was a shepherd Isaiah is described in Isaiah 2.1 as 'the son of Amoz': Hogg is perhaps confusing the identity of 'Amoz' with the prophet Amos, who described how God chose him as a prophet as he 'followed the flock' in Amos 7.14-15.

16(d) his inherent vanity Hogg establishes two well-known aspects of his public personality, vanity and an affection for the other sex. R. P. Gillies relates that his vanity was 'avowed and undisguised, and he himself laughed at it objectively as such. It never, for one instant appeared to me as arrogance or self-conceit; on the contrary, it was mere native eccentricity, or in better words, decision of character'—see R.P. Gillies, *Memoirs of a Literary Veteran*, 3 vols (London, 1851), II, 128-29. Near the start of his autobiography Hogg declares outright, 'I have liked the women a great deal better than the men ever since I remember'—see *Memoir*, p.6.

16(d)–17(a) a false and defective education in Hogg's lifetime his own eldest daughter, Janet Phillips Hogg, seems to have received a similar formal education to her brother James. In her letter of 11 February 1832, written to her husband during his London visit, Hogg's wife reports their children's progress at school as follows: 'Jessy is rather before Jas at the Latin but both are I believe learning well & Maggie is improving in reading'—see Parr, p.103.

20(a) *coup de main* a sudden stroke, or stratagem by which something is effected suddenly.

20(b) sanguine hopeful or confident, the characteristics of a person of a complexion in which blood predominated over the other three humours in medieval medicine.

21(a) circulating libraries commercial lending libraries, common in Hogg's day and so called because the books circulated among the subscribers. They were often viewed by moralists as corrupting young women by purveying sensational reading matter in a way that eluded the supervision of their parents and guardians. Hogg's comments here are made within the context of the morally-improving essay-periodical tradition.

21(b) Ladies' novels Hogg is presumably complaining about fiction written by women which, in his eyes, was over-concerned with the particularities of fashionable manners and decorum. His complaints about Blackwood's treatment of him in the early 1830s include postponing his own magazine articles to make way for 'feminine frible-frable' (see an undated letter from Hogg to Blackwood, in NLS, MS 4029, fol.27) and 'wretched lady articles' (see the letter from Hogg to John Wilson of 16 March 1833, in NLS, MS 2530, fols.3-4). Despite these complaints his own interest in female fiction is demonstrated in *The Three Perils of Woman* (1823).

21(b) two at present living one of the ladies' novelists excepted by Hogg from general censure was Susan Ferrier (1782-1854), whose *Marriage* (1818) and *The Inheritance* (1824) he praised enthusiastically in a letter to William Blackwood of 28 June 1824, in NLS, MS 4012, fols.184-85. A third novel by Ferrier, *Destiny*, had been published in 1831.

21(d) the greatest [...] novelist that ever was born while it is impossible to be certain to whom Hogg refers here, it may perhaps be to Samuel Richardson (1689-1761), who was disturbed that the heartless villain Lovelace in his *Clarissa Harlowe* (1747-48) had become an object of pity to his female readers, some of whom censured his heroine for refusing to marry him. On 26 October 1748 he wrote to Lady Bradshaigh, 'it has been matter of Surprize to me, and indeed of some Concern, that this Character has met with so much Favour from the good and the virtuous'—see *Selected Letters of Samuel Richardson*, ed. by John Carroll (Oxford: Clarendon Press, 1964), p.92.

22(b) *memento mori* in Latin, 'remember you must die'; a phrase often referring to an emblem to put a person in remembrance of the shortness and uncertainty of life, such as a skull.

22(b) Romances originally a verse tale about the life and adventures of a hero of chivalry, but by Hogg's time a fictitious prose narrative of which the scene and incidents are remote from ordinary life, often with the implication of extravagance and exaggeration. Hogg is at his most negative here, but his *The Three Perils of Man* (1822) is described on its title-page as 'A Border Romance'.

22(d) The road [...] thickets of briers and thorns [...] meadows of flowers a proverbial contrast of the broad way leading to damnation and the narrow way leading to salvation, recalling Matthew 7.13-14: 'Enter ye in at the strait gate: for wide is the gate, and broad is the way, which leadeth to destruction [...] strait is the gate, and narrow is the way, which leadeth unto life'. Hogg's heroine Cherry Elliot has a dream in which she follows 'a winding-path through flowery shrubs' to a fall from a precipice: the dream prefigures her early death of a broken heart—see *The Three Perils of Woman*, ed. by David Groves, Antony Hasler, and Douglas S. Mack (Edinburgh: Edinburgh University Press, 1995), p.27.

23(a) "wisdom [...] get understanding." see Proverbs 4.7.

23(d) Lord Byron or Anacreon Moore the poetry of George Gordon, Lord Byron (1788-1824) was immensely popular but much criticised on moral grounds, while Thomas Moore (1779-1852) published in 1800 a translation of the odes of Anacreon, a lyric poet of the 6th century BC who wrote verses on love and wine. Presumably Hogg reinforces ironically here his earlier point about miscellaneous reading for young ladies.

25(c) the feast of reason 'The feast of reason and the flow of soul', Alexander Pope, *Epistles and Satires of Horace Imitated. To Mr Fortescue*, line 128.

26(c) Sterne's Laurence Sterne (1713-68), the author of *Tristram Shandy*, published in all seven volumes of sermons; the first two volumes, *Sermons of Mr Yorick*, appeared in 1760.

26(c) Boston's the theologian Thomas Boston (1677-1732) was a revered figure in Hogg's native Ettrick, of which he had been minister from 1707 until his death in 1732.

26(d) Leviticus is the third book of the old testament, and, as Hogg says, concerned with Jewish ritual law.

27(b) "Remember now thy Creator [...] youth." Ecclesiastes 12.1.

Sermon III. Good Breeding
text Proverbs 15.4.

28(b) the great moral philosopher of Israel the book of Proverbs is said to be the work of King Solomon (Proverbs 1.1).

28(c) the gift of tongues without charity from II Corinthians 13.1, 'Though I speak with the tongues of men and of angels, and have not charity, I am become as sounding brass, or a tinkling cymbal'.

28(d) the brink of science an allusion to Alexander Pope, *An Essay on Criticism*, lines 215-16: 'A *little Learning* is a dang'rous Thing;/ Drink deep, or taste not the *Pierian* Spring'.

29(a) Sir Walter Scott [...] check my loquacity compare the similar statement in Hogg's *Familiar Anecdotes*, p.113: 'I must confess that before people of high rank he did not much encourage my speeches and stories. [...] he generally cut me short by some droll anecdote to the same purport of what I was saying. In this he did not give me fair justice for in my own broad homely way I am a very good speaker and teller of a story too'.

29(b) Professor Wilson's see the earlier note to 14(d).

29(b) Wordsworth see Hogg's own parody of Wordsworth, 'The Stranger; being a farther portion of "The Recluse, A Poem" ', in *The Poetic Mirror* (London, 1816), pp.133-53. Wilson, 'he of the Palmy Isle', responds to one of Wordsworth's philosophical rhapsodies by looking in his face 'and ever and anon/ He utter'd a short sound at every pause,/ But further ventured not—' (p.151).

29(c) Mrs. G–, Miss B–, and Mrs. S– [...] **Mrs. J–** even to contemporaries the identities of these literary ladies were not obvious, one critic describing himself as 'quite at fault' here—see *Fraser's Magazine*, 10 (July 1834), 1-10 (p.8). Hogg clearly does not give enough detail for his reader to identify them in more than a speculative fashion. However, it is possible that 'Mrs. G–' may be Anne Grant of Laggan (1755-1838), the author of *Letters from the Mountains* (1806) and a well-known Edinburgh hostess and blue-stocking, for she visited her 'old acquaintance the Ettrick Shepherd' at Altrive in August 1833—see Parr, pp.121-22. It is also possible that 'Miss B–' is the Scottish poet and playwright Joanna Baillie (1762-1851): Hogg probably met her in 1820 while she was staying with Scott at Abbotsford, for his letter to William Blackwood of 12 October (in NLS, MS 4005, fol.166) reveals that he expected a visit from her during the following week. Her house at Hampstead was the meeting-place of a lively literary circle, and it may be that the acquaintance was renewed during Hogg's London visit of 1832. 'Mrs. J–' may possibly represent Christian Isobel Johnstone (1781-1857), the author of *Clan-Albin, A National Tale* (1815) and *Elizabeth de Bruce* (1827), as well as various children's books and a cookery book purporting to be the work of Meg Dods of Scott's *St. Ronan's Well*—see Virginia Blain, Patricia Clemens, and Isobel Grundy, *The Feminist Companion to Literature in English: Women Writers from the Middle Ages to the Present* (London: B. T. Batsford, 1990), pp.585-86.

29(d) president the person who occupies the chief place at table, and superintends or directs.

29(d) Dr. Barclay, of Edinburgh John Barclay (1758-1826) was an anatomist in Edinburgh from 1797 to 1825, giving regular lectures to students every winter session. In 1804 he was formally recognised as a lecturer by the Edinburgh College of Surgeons, and in 1806 became a fellow of the Edinburgh College of Physicians. The infamous Dr Robert Knox had been one of his pupils, and took over his work when his health failed in the final year of his life.

30(b) London Hogg's experience of London society was confined to a single stay, which took place during the first three months of 1832, when he was feted as one of the literary lions of the season. Hogg gave further impressions of this visit in his 'Noctes Ambrosianae New Series No 2', ed. by Douglas S. Mack and G. H. Hughes, in *Altrive Chapbooks*, 2 (1985), 30-54, where he is described as 'shown off to every large party in town like a wild beast of extraordinary dimensions' (p.44).

30(b) Allan Cunningham Hogg first met the writer Allan Cunningham (1784-1842) when he was a shepherd at Mitchelslacks in Nithsdale. Hogg relates in his *Memoir* (pp.71-73) how the young Cunningham, accompanied by his elder brother James, a stone-mason at Dalswinton, came to pay his respects and introduce himself to the shepherd-poet. Cunningham was the chief contributor to Cromek's *Remains of Nithsdale and Galloway Song* (1810), and was subsequently introduced to the sculptor Francis Chantrey, who employed him for many years in London as secretary and superintendent of his works. He published a number of prose fictions, and also the *Traditional Tales of the English and Scottish Peasantry* (1822) and *The Songs of Scotland, Ancient and Modern* (1825). Hogg contributed to the *Anniversary*, an Annual edited by Cunningham, and their friendship continued until Hogg's death.

30(c) Captain Selby [...] **Mr Walker, your friend** unfortunately Hogg does not provide enough information to identify these men.

30(d) **Mr. H–t's** the name of Hogg's host on this occasion is unknown.

31(d) **our ideas partake of material substance** the origin of this theory has not been identified. From the time of Descartes ideas were generally defined as things that exist only as the contents of some minds. While Plato's Greek word *idea* (which is more accurately translated as 'form') does suggest something which exists apart from any conscious being, this is still not a material object.

32(b) **a lady who mentioned the term *indelicate*** similar sentiments are expressed at the conclusion of 'Part Fifth' of Hogg's poem *Queen Hynde*, 'Such word or term should never be/ In maiden's mind of modesty'.

33(c) **Croly** Rev. George Croly (1780-1860) was settled in London as a poet and periodical writer. He contributed chiefly to *Blackwood's Edinburgh Magazine*, and the *Literary Gazette*, and is perhaps best known as the author of the novel *Salathiel* (1828). Elsewhere Hogg refers to 'Croly wi his true logical eloquence'–see 'Noctes Ambrosiane New Series No 2', ed. by Douglas S. Mack and G. H. Hughes, in *Altrive Chapbooks*, 2 (1985), 30-54 (pp.35-36).

33(c) **Hood** Thomas Hood (1799-1845), the poet and humorist, was brother-in-law to John Hamilton Reynolds, also mentioned here by Hogg. His best-known poem in 1834 was probably 'Eugene Aram's Dream'. He had written to Hogg on 22 April 1828 asking him to become a contributor to his Annual *The Gem*–see NLS, MS 2245, fol.116.

33(c) **Reynolds** John Hamilton Reynolds (1796-1852), a poet and friend of Keats, was a contributor to the *Athenaeum*, and a proprietor until 1831.

33(c) **Hook** Theodore Hook (1788-1841) was the editor of *John Bull* and the author of nine volumes of fiction under the heading of *Sayings and Doings* (1826-29); he was also well-known among his contemporaries for his social skills, wit, and practical jokes.

33(c) **Martin** John Martin (1789-1854), the fashionable painter of historical scenes and landscapes in which human figures are dwarfed by colossal scenery and buildings. His pictures included 'The Fall of Babylon' (1819), 'Belshazzer's Feast' (1821), and 'The Fall of Nineveh' (1833). His pictures were engraved and reproduced in the Annuals, where they were admired by the young Brontës as well as by Hogg. In a letter to his wife of 10 January 1832, after meeting Martin the previous evening, Hogg refers to him as 'the sublime painter'–see Garden, p.247. Hogg evidently corresponded with Martin after his London visit, and Martin's letter to him of 29 May 1833 (in NLS, MS 2245, fols.222-23) indicates that he had produced a drawing illustrating a passage from Hogg's most popular poem 'Kilmeny' in which the artist's daughter Isabelle seems to have been the model for the heroine.

33(c) **Cruikshanks** George Cruikshank (1792-1878) made his name by drawing and etching social and political caricatures, but in the 1820s turned to book illustration, being best-remembered now for his illustrations to the early work of Dickens. Hogg's *Altrive Tales* (1832) contains an illustration by Cruikshank, and Cruikshank was among Hogg's hosts during his London visit in 1832–see Garden, p.246.

33(c) **Among the nobility and gentry** in his 'Memoir of Burns' Hogg explains that a poet belongs to no particular class of society, and compares himself with Burns: 'I, like him, was a son of the lowly cot, and among the shepherds and cottagers I am happy to this day. [...] Again, in the society of farmers, I am one of them; we are all as brothers; and among the first nobility of the land I am equally at my ease: so that really I feel I belong exclusively to no one class of society'–see *The Works of Robert Burns*, ed. by James Hogg and William Motherwell, 5 vols (Glasgow, 1834-36), V, 192.

34(d) blue-stockings literary or learned ladies.

35(a) Mr. Holmes William Jerdan describes how after dinner at the Chief of the Macleods' house during Hogg's London visit the fun was suddenly interrupted by one gentleman who 'jumped up from his chair, and laying almost violent hands upon several other gentlemen, hurried them reluctantly out of the room, with the bare assurance that there was a hackney-coach at the door that would hold six! That individual was Billy Holmes, the occasion an unlooked-for division and hurried whip, and the forcibly abducted convives Warrenders, Gordons, Cummings [...]'—see William Jerdan, *Autobiography*, 4 vols (London, 1852-53), IV, 298-99. Hogg clearly thought that William Holmes, the Tory whip, was rather arbitrary in his attempts to get the Scottish M.P.s dining with him at Macleod's off to the House of Commons. Macleod invited Hogg to dine with him on 15 February 1832 at 100 Great Cumberland Street—see his letter to Hogg of 1 February 1832, in NLS, MS 2245, fol.187.

35(d) beet radish beetroot.

35(d) arcana hidden things or secret mysteries.

36(d) retire from the world after his illness at the beginning of 1833 Hogg seems to have been more at home than ever before. He went to Edinburgh with Charles Marshall in the last year of his life and, as Marshall relates, 'so long a period had elapsed since he was much in the metropolis, that with the exception of Robert Chambers, John Johnstone, and a few others, no one recognised him'—see Garden, p.305. An attitude of retirement from the evils of the town, by dwelling in the wilderness of the Borders, was nevertheless often affected by Hogg in earlier years. In a letter to William Blackwood of 12 August 1816 (in NLS, MS 4001, fol. 209), for instance, he states that 'the most graceful way of giving up the contest is to retire indignant into my native glens and consort with the rustic friends of my early youth'.

37(d) Deists people who accept the existence of a God on rational grounds, but reject revealed religion.

38(d) the great King of Israel Proverbs 1.1 states that this book of the bible contains the 'proverbs of Solomon the son of David, king of Israel'.

38(d) "A word fitly [...] pictures of silver." Proverbs 25.11.

38(d) "The words of the wise [...] the assemblies." see Ecclesiastes 12.11.

38(d) "Let [...] use of edifying." see Ephesians 4.29.

38(d) "Be ye filled [...] mutually." this quotation has not been precisely identified, though the phrase 'be filled with the Spirit' is in Ephesians 5.18, and there is also possibly an allusion to Romans 1.11-12: 'For I long to see you, that I may impart unto you some spiritual gifts, to the end ye may be established; That is, that I may be comforted together with you by the mutual faith both of you and me'.

38(d)–39(a) "Let the word of Christ [...] admonishing one another." Colossians 3.16.

Sermon IV. Soldiers

text see James 4.1 for the first sentence: the second sentence is Acts 7.26, with 'harm' substituted for 'wrong'.

40(b) to do justly, to love mercy, walk humbly see Micah 6.8.

40(b) made upright [...] many inventions see Ecclesiastes 7.29.

40(c) pass the Rubicon to take a decisive step—Caesar's crossing the river Rubicon in the north of Italy marked the beginning of his war with Pompey.

41(c) all their imperfections on their heads see *Hamlet*, I.5.79.

41(d) the campaigns of Buonaparte by 1810 Napoleon Bonaparte (1769-1821) had formed a French empire by a brilliant series of military conquests (1805-09), covering most of Europe with the exception of Russia. This empire ended only with the repartition of Europe after his defeat at Waterloo in 1815. Hogg's comment illustrates the force of the impact of the Napoleonic wars on the nineteenth century, comparable to that of the European war of 1914-1918 on the twentieth century.

42(a) a scene I once saw in Nithsdale Hogg later refers at p.44(a) to this Nithsdale incident as taking place more specifically at Thornhill: between 1805 and 1810 he had been firstly a shepherd at Mitchelslacks and then a farmer at Locherben, dating his letters from both farms 'by Thornhill' in Dumfriesshire. The incident presumably dates from this period of his life.

42(a) glowrin' scowling.

42(a) daur to dare or venture.

42(b) coped came to blows, met in battle.

42(d) champion, like the Israelites and Philistines Hogg is probably thinking of the challenge issued to the Israelites by Goliath of Gath on behalf of the Philistines in I Samuel 17.8-10. The young David accepted the challenge on behalf of the Israelites and defeated Goliath.

42(d) sentiments of King David see I Samuel 24.17 and I Chronicles 21.17.

43(d) the strength and the courage of Hector Hector was the eldest son of Priam, the Trojan king in Homer's *Iliad*, and the bravest of the Trojan chieftains.

44(a) nation against nation in Matthew 24.7 Jesus describes the events before the end of the world as including wars, when 'nation shall rise up against nation, and kingdom against kingdom'.

44(a) boy of Thornhill's terms see note to 42(a).

44(d) the soldiers came to John the Baptist the incident and quotation are from Luke 3.14.

45(a) "I have not found [...] in Israel." the quotation is from Luke 7.9. A centurion asked Jesus to heal his servant, saying that Jesus's word would be sufficient without his physical presence at the sick-bed.

45(a) "the law of nations." this phrase, denoting the common rules of agreement or custom by which nations are bound together as part of a single society, dates back at least as far as the end of the seventeenth century.

46(a) the Turks and Tartars the inhabitants of Turkey and of central Asia are still referred to as unmanageably violent and savage in such expressions as 'a little Turk' or 'to catch a Tartar'.

46(b–c) "The wolf [...] cover the sea." see Isaiah 11.6-9. Hogg omits from verse 9 the phrase 'They shall not hurt nor destroy in all my holy mountain'. A *cockatrice* is a mythical reptile, a serpent hatched from a cock's egg.

46(d) that the sword may not devour for ever a phrase used by Abner to Joab in asking for a cessation of hostilities in II Samuel 2.26.

47(a) unleash the dogs [...] of war in allusion to Shakespeare's *Julius Caesar*, III.1.276: 'Cry "havoc!" and let slip the dogs of war'.

47(b) the second man [...] the first murder alluding to Cain's murder of his brother Abel in Genesis 4.8. Cain, as Adam's elder son, was the second man to be born in the world.

47(b–c) "The dreadful harass [...] slumbers o'er her prey." see Nicholas Rowe, *Tamerlane, a Tragedy*, II.1.1-6. In printed editions of the play the word 'harass' in the first line reads 'Business'.

Sermon V. To Young Men

text Proverbs 1.10.

48(c) after the year 1813 Hogg only became widely recognised as a writer after the publication of *The Queen's Wake* in 1813. R. P. Gillies says that 'till then Hogg had only been talked of as an eccentric being, uncouth and rude in manners, who had written divers clever songs and ballads, which appeared in magazines and newspapers. But the "Queen's Wake" instantly lifted him up to an entirely new and unexpected grade on the Scottish Parnassus'—see *Memoirs of a Literary Veteran*, 3 vols (London, 1851), II, 122.

48(c) gloveless hand a gentleman would wear gloves but not a person engaged in a manual occupation, such as a shepherd.

48(c) "Go thy ways, Paul," perhaps a reference to the words of Felix to Paul in Acts 24.25, 'Go thy way for this time; when I have a convenient season, I will call for thee'.

50(c) Lavater Johann Kaspar Lavater (1741-1801) was the Swiss inventor of physiognomy, which claimed to be able to interpret character from the physical aspect of the face.

50(c) Spurzheim Johann Kaspar Spurzheim (1776-1832) was a writer on phrenology, who interpreted the conformation of a man's skull as an index to his mental and moral qualities. Lockhart reported that when Hogg's own head was examined by Dr Spurzheim the Shepherd jestingly compared these intellectual protuberances with the swellings and bruises that resulted from a fight at a country fair: 'My dear fellow, [...] if a few knots and swells make a skull of genius, I've seen mony a saft chield get a swapping organization in five minutes at Selkirk tryst.'—see *Peter's Letters to his Kinsfolk*, 3 vols (Edinburgh, 1819), II, 341.

51(b) "Let no such man be trusted" see Shakespeare's *The Merchant of Venice*, V.1.88. Hogg also uses this motto in the first sermon of his collection—see p.12(a) and note.

52(b) there is a way [...] destruction another reference to Matthew 7.13-14. See also p.22(d) and note.

52(d) Satan [...] an angel of light the well-known legend that Satan, the great adversary of mankind, was an archangel before being cast out of heaven for rebellion is perhaps connected with his name of Lucifer, meaning 'bringing light'.

53(b) the wicked [...] pursueth an allusion to Proverbs 28.1.

54(b) the friends thou hast [...] hoops of steel an allusion to Polonius's advice to his son Laertes in Shakespeare's *Hamlet*, I.3.62-63.

54(c) One of the old English poets the poet and the quotation which follow have not been identified.

55(a) this blessing of infinite price perhaps an echo of the 'pearl of great price' of Matthew 13.45-46.

56(b) Professor John Wilson see note to 14(d).

56(c) imitate me save the professor himself another reference to John Wilson's role as one of the authors of the 'Noctes Ambrosianae' of *Blackwood's Edinburgh Magazine*, in which Hogg appeared in the strongly-caricatured form of the Shepherd—see note to 14(d).

Sermon VI. Reason and Instinct
text 1 Thessalonians 5.23.

58(c) Philosophers [...] its seat in the body the French philosopher René Descartes (1596-1650) held that the soul would be powerless to influence the body unless some part of the brain could transmit and receive its signals, and fixed upon the pineal gland as performing this function.

58(c) my [...] patron Dr. Dunlop Dr William Dunlop was the person to whom *Lay Sermons* was dedicated—for information about him see the note to the dedication.

58(c) the ancients have supposed the Greek philosopher Aristotle (364-322 BC) argued that there are three souls, or ways of functioning: a plant has a soul as it feeds and reproduces; an animal can additionally move and sense; and a person besides these has the capacity to think.

59(d) studied [...] animals Hogg's employment in his youth as a shepherd would obviously bring him into daily and hourly contact with sheep and dogs.

60(a) a shepherd's dog some of Hogg's observations on his own dogs are embodied in his articles 'Further Anecdotes of the Shepherd's Dog' and 'The Shepherd's Calendar. Class IV. Dogs', in *Blackwood's Edinburgh Magazine*, 2 (March 1818), 621-26 and 15 (February 1824), 177-83 respectively.

60(b) Mr. Paton Charles Paton was minister of Ettrick from 8 December 1791 until his death on 18 February 1818. He died unmarried at the age of 63.

60(b) yaud an old mare or worn-out horse.

60(c) Solomon see Ecclesiastes 3.21. Solomon is referred to as the author of Ecclesiastes in 1.1: 'The Words of the Preacher, the son of David, king in Jerusalem'.

61(d) reason, speech, or risibility reason, language, and laughter are the three most usual ways of distinguishing men from animals. Aristotle was probably the first philosopher to maintain that rationality is the key distinction between man and other animals.

62(d) wives of a nabob the reference to polygamy suggests that Hogg is using *nabob* in its original sense of a muslim deputy-governor of a district under the Mogul empire in India, rather than in the contemporary sense of a European returned from India with a large fortune.

62(d) Wordsworth says the quotation has not been identified in Wordsworth's poetry, though Hogg uses it in his Wordsworth parody, 'The Stranger; being a farther portion of "The Recluse, A Poem" ', in *The Poetic Mirror*, (London, 1816), pp.133-53 (p.149): 'it is known/ To many, and not quite to me unknown,/ That the youth's heart is better than his head'.

63(b) a Cameronian sacrament Cameronians were originally the followers of Richard Cameron (1648-1680), a covenanting extremist. They held that the Church of Scotland as established in 1690 during the reign of William and Mary was unacceptable because it compromised with the state, and in 1743 constituted their own Reformed Presbyterian Church.

64(b) convolvolous Hogg's own word, probably derived either from *convolving*, meaning coiling and twisting, or from *convulvulus*, the bindweed.

64(c) organisation the connection or co-ordination of parts for vital funtions; the bodily constitution.

64(d) until once death was overcome through the crucifixion and resurrection of Jesus.

64(d) lives, moves, and hath its being see Acts 17.28.

65(a) bodily eyes [...] begin to see a passage based perhaps on I Corinthians 13.12.

65(b) arrows of liquid flame [...] thunder perhaps a reminiscence of Psalm 77.17-18: 'thine arrows also went abroad. The voice of thy thunder was in the heaven'.

65(c) "to follow nature up to nature's God." see Alexander Pope, 'An Essay on Man', line 332, 'But looks through nature up to nature's God'.

65(d) his own image see Genesis 1.27, where after the creation of animals God 'created man in his own image'.

66(c) clay tabernacle i.e. the human body as the temporary dwelling-place of the soul.

67(a) clods of the valley an expression derived from Job 21.33.

67(a) house not made with hands II Corinthians 5.1: 'For we know that if our earthly house of this tabernacle were dissolved, we have a building of God, an house not made with hands, eternal in the heavens'.

Sermon VII. To Parents
text Proverbs 22.6.

68(b) felt the want of it his father's financial failure meant that Hogg himself was sent out as a herd at seven years of age and had almost no formal schooling—see *Memoir*, p.5.

68(b) since the building of Babel see Genesis 11.1-9. The people of Babel tried to build a tower the top of which would reach heaven, but to prevent their co-operation in this project God scattered them and introduced different languages among them.

70(b) a second time into the fire alluding to the proverb, 'A burnt child dreads the fire'—see *The Oxford Dictionary of English Proverbs*, third edition, rev. by F. P. Wilson (Oxford: Clarendon Press, 1970), p.92.

70(c) I dare not altogether condemn it perhaps a jocular reference to Solomon. The text for this sermon is one of Solomon's maxims on the subject of child-rearing, but his 'He that spareth his rod hateth his son' (Proverbs 13.21) is much better known.

72(b) several printed plans of education the best-known books on the education of children were probably John Locke's *Some Thoughts Concerning Education* (1693) and Jean Jacques Rousseau's *Émile* (1762), though Hogg may have seen more recent works such as Maria and Richard Lovell Edgeworth's *Essays on Practical Education* (1798) and Elizabeth Hamilton's *Letters on Education* (1801-02). Rousseau's plan certainly supposed 'feeling and attention on the part of parents which are not to be found in the world', for the father (or tutor substituting for him) was to be the constant companion and sole director of the child night and day from his birth to the age of twenty-five. Rousseau, however, did not advocate alms-giving by children and his emphasis is on the effect on the giver rather than the recipient of charity.

72(d) the tales for children among the best-known authors of moral tales for children, a common form of publication from about 1800, were Maria Edgeworth, the author of *Moral Tales* and *Early Lessons* (1801), and Mary Martha Sherwood, the author of *The Fairchild Family* (1818).

74(a) Adam Neil nothing is known of this man.

74(b) stithy anvil.

74(b) Richmond Place is in the university district of Edinburgh, parallel to Nicolson Street.

74(c) Elibank [...] Willenslee these farms belonged to a son and father named Laidlaw, whom Hogg served as a farm-labourer and shepherd in his adolescence—see *Memoir*, p.8.

74(d) another quiet remote place 'At Whitsunday 1790, being still only in the eighteenth year of my age, I left Willenslee, and hired myself to Mr. Laidlaw of Black House, with whom I served as a shepherd ten years'—see *Memoir*, p.9.

75(d) training young fruit-trees to a wall perhaps an allusion to Matthew 12.33: 'Either make the tree good, and his fruit good; or else make the tree corrupt, and his fruit corrupt: for the tree is known by his fruit'. Hogg may also have in mind James Thomson's 'Spring' (lines 1152-53) from *The Seasons*, 'Delightful task! to rear the tender thought,/ To teach the young idea how to shoot'.

75(d) limber easily bent, flexible or supple.

76(b) the charge of a considerable [...] family Hogg had five children by his marriage to Margaret Phillips: James Robert (born 1821), Janet Phillips (born 1823), Margaret Laidlaw (born 1825), Harriet Sidney (born 1827), and Mary Gray (born 1831). Family was often used, however, in the wider sense of household.

76(c) walk in his ways Moses was commanded by God to tell the Israelites to 'walk in all the ways which the Lord your God hath commanded you' in Deuteronomy 5.33.

76(d) college education the function of the Scottish universities was a hotly-

debated issue in the 1820s and 1830s. In 1826 a Royal Commission had been
appointed to look at the Universities of Scotland, which because of the influence
of presbyterianism had evolved differently from those of England. Students entered university at the early age of fifteen or sixteen and were given a four years'
general education, including classics, science, and compulsory philosophy. The
more able or more wealthy students would then undertake professional studies
afterwards, for example in law or divinity. The Report produced by the Royal
Commission in 1831 favoured moving the Scottish universities towards the English model, but nothing was done about it because of fierce national feeling in
favour of Scotland's own system—see George Elder Davie, *The Democratic Intellect:
Scotland and her Universities in the Nineteenth Century* (Edinburgh: Edinburgh University Press, 1961, repr. 1981), pp.3-38.

Hogg's later references to 'ancient and modern history, astronomy, and geography' (p.78) and 'botany and chemistry' (p.79) as useful studies, seem to indicate that he is in favour of neither system but of a more general education still,
and one that is specifically geared to the student's later life or professional interests.

77(a) **our colleges [...] founded and established so long ago** Hogg is presumably
referring to the Scottish universities: St Andrews (founded 1412), Glasgow
(founded 1451), King's College, Aberdeen (founded 1495), Edinburgh (founded
1583), and Marischal College, Aberdeen (founded 1593). Hogg would have
been most familiar with the post-Reformation foundation of Edinburgh.

77(b) **two whole sessions are consumed** at the University of Edinburgh in Hogg's
day students got a double dose of philosophy, especially of the theory of knowledge, that is perception, universals, and causality. During one year they would
attend the Logic class, during which some formal logic would be combined with
an outline of the theory of knowledge, and during the following year they would
attend the Moral Philosophy class, during which ethics would be combined with
a more elaborate discussion of the theory of knowledge—see George Elder Davie,
The Democratic Intellect: Scotland and her Universities in the Nineteenth Century (Edinburgh: Edinburgh University Press, 1961, repr. 1981), p.11.

77(d) **the schools** an expression of medieval origin, referring to the scholastic philosophers and theologians collectively, and subsequently applied to the faculties
of a university. Hogg is reinforcing his point about the restricted education ob-
tainable in an institution originating with the medieval church.

78(a) **crabbed questions and metaphysical jargon** the predominance of philosophy in the Scottish curriculum meant that it was 'the first of the higher subjects in
which students would receive a thorough grounding and become intellectually
confident. Coming to the University at the age of fifteen or sixteen without much
knowledge of any subject but Latin [...] they thus found themselves able to argue
about Hume's theory of causality and about Berkeley's theory of perception in
the very years in which in their Greek and their mathematical classes they were
still doing very elementary work'—see George Elder Davie, *The Democratic Intellect: Scotland and her Universities in the Nineteenth Century* (Edinburgh: Edinburgh
University Press, 1961, repr. 1981), p.12.

Davie also indicates that the predominance of philosophy was also felt in other
areas of the curriculum, in that students were introduced to the general principles
of a subject before its practical details (p.14).

78(b) **One contends** St Thomas Aquinas (1224\5-74) identified moral principles
with God's commands.

78(b) **another** the proponent of the theory that morality is founded in conformity to
truth has not been identified.

78(c) **a third** the English metaphysician Samuel Clarke (1675-1729) argued that moral judgements can be as certain as mathematical judgements: a correct judgement is one which is appropriate to a given situation, so that, for example, we feel grateful when we have received a favour.

78(c) a fourth the Scottish moral philosopher Francis Hutcheson (1694-1746/7) was the chief proponent of the 'moral sense' basis of morality, emphasising feeling rather than reason as the basis of judgement.

78(c) another the Scottish philosopher David Hume (1711-76) based the foundation of morality on 'sympathy', the power of sharing the unhappiness or pleasure of others.

78(c) "Words! words!" as Hamlet says see *Hamlet*, II. 2. 195.

78(d) a highly-esteemed friend of my own John Wilson–see note to 14(d).

79(c) "They gang in [...] asses;" see Burns, 'Epistle to J. L–k, An Old Scotch Bard', line 69. A *stirk* is a young bullock kept for slaughter or, by transference, an oaf.

79(d) the professors [...] keep at too great a distance this was to some extent inevitable in view of the size of some of their classes. From figures submitted to the Royal Commission it would appear that between 1820 and 1825 the philosophy classes at both Edinburgh and Glasgow each averaged about 150 students. The professor would give formal lectures, and often supplement these with examination hours in which he questioned students round the class on the subject of the lecture. Several essays would be set during the course, and passages from some of these would also be read and debated during the examination hours. Hogg's friend John Wilson, when Professor of Moral Philosophy at Edinburgh, went over his students' essays at a public discussion held on Saturdays, which sometimes lasted from noon to three p.m.–see George Elder Davie, *The Democratic Intellect: Scotland and her Universities in the Nineteenth Century* (Edinburgh: Edinburgh University Press, 1961, repr. 1981), pp.19, 14, 17. Clearly with such large classes it was not possible for even the best-intentioned professors to pay much attention to the individual requirements of their students.

79(d) far too many classes students attended university during the winter months, selecting their own classes and then paying the appropriate fee for each one (in Edinburgh usually three guineas, or £3.15, for literary and philosophical subjects). Even though few students actually graduated most would study the seven subjects prescribed for the M.A. degree: Latin and Greek, Logic and Moral Philosophy, Mathematics and Natural Philosophy, with one of the languages or Mathematics additionally studied at a higher level. For most purposes the 'class ticket' was sufficient evidence of the student's proficiency, a testimonial of the student's attendance and diligence signed by the professor. This course of study would normally take four years–see Laurance J. Saunders, *Scottish Democracy 1815-1840: The Social and Intellectual Background* (Edinburgh and London: Oliver & Boyd, 1950), pp.307-08, 353, 361. Hogg's remark may indicate that he thought the study of these seven subjects in four years placed too heavy a burden on young men who were studying only during the winter months and recruiting their finances during the other half of the year. It may also be possible that poorer students were tempted to shorten the course by taking more classes per winter session than usual.

80(a) fear, nurture, and admonition of the Lord Paul instructs fathers in Ephesians 6.4 to bring up their children 'in the nurture and admonition of the Lord'.

80(b) all the days of their lives an expression found in several places in the Bible.

Sermon VIII. Virtue the Only Source of Happiness
text Psalm 144.15.

82(a) the thousand ills that flesh is heir to *Hamlet*, III.1.64-65, 'the thousand natural shocks/ That flesh is heir to'.

82(d) **upwards of twenty years [...] all classes of society** Hogg again dates his introduction into genteel society as having occurred after the publication of *The Queen's Wake* in 1813: compare his statement on p.48(c). As Hogg did not become famous until he was in his forties his youth was passed among the shepherds, as he says.

83(a) **shepherd [...] the ward of Heaven** Hogg expresses a similar sense of the shepherd's dependence upon God as the ruler of the elements in 'Storms', in *The Shepherd's Calendar*, ed. by Douglas S. Mack (Edinburgh: Edinburgh University Press, 1995), pp.3-4.

85(d) **contentment with little** perhaps an echo of Robert Burns's song beginning 'Contented wi' little, and cantie wi' mair'.

85(d) **house to house, and field to field** an allusion to Isaiah 5.8: 'Woe unto them that join house to house, that lay field to field [...]'.

85(d) **vanity and vexation of spirit** an allusion to Ecclesiastes 2.11, 'all was vanity and vexation of spirit, and there was no profit under the sun'.

86(a) **the wise man** Solomon, the author of the book of Ecclesiastes.

86(a) **"I hated all my labour [...] good before God."** see Ecclesiastes 2.18-19, 26.

86(a) **"There is one alone [...] travail."** see Ecclesiastes 4.8.

86(b) **the great King of Israel** Solomon.

86(b) **the wives, concubines, and virgins [...] one son, and he was a fool** see I Kings 11.3, 'And he had seven hundred wives, princesses, and three hundred concubines'. Solomon's son Rehoboam ignored the advice of his counsellors to deal gently with the complaints of the Israelites and lost most of his kingdom to Jereboam—see I Kings 12.1-20.

86(c) **his moral instructions [...] definitions of happiness** the beatitudes in the Sermon on the Mount, which include those on the meek, the merciful and the pure in heart—see Matthew 5.1-12.

87(a) **that good which he can find under the sun** an expression much repeated in Ecclesiastes: it occurs, for instance, three times in the first chapter alone, at verses 3, 9, and 14.

87(a) **maxim is three times repeated** the quotation is from Ecclesiastes 2.24, and similar expressions occur at 3.13 and 5.18.

87(c) **"Whatsoever [...] all hastening."** see Ecclesiastes 9.10; quoted inexactly here, presumably from memory.

88(c) **With God all things are possible** a phrase derived from Matthew 19.26.

88(d) **the polar star** Polaris, or the pole star, is about one degree from the northern pole of the heavens and was therefore commonly used as an indication of direction at night by sailors and by country-folk such as shepherds.

89(a) **ambrosia** in Greek mythology the food of the gods, which made them immortal.

89(b) **a great evil under the sun** see Ecclesiastes 5.13: 'There is a sore evil which I have seen under the sun, namely, riches kept for the owners thereof to their hurt'.

89(c) **Alexander wept when he had no more worlds to conquer** Alexander the Great, or Alexander III of Macedon (356-323 BC), the subject of much literature and legend. This particular phrase had become something of a tired commonplace by the nineteenth century. As Dickens later remarked in the second chapter of *Bleak House*: 'How Alexander wept when he had no more worlds to conquer, everybody knows—or has some reason to know by this time, the matter having been rather frequently mentioned'—see *Bleak House*, Oxford Illustrated Dickens (Oxford: Oxford University Press, 1948, reprinted 1981), p.10.

89(d) **well known in what a labyrinth of poverty and toil** the three versions of *Memoir of the Author's Life* published in 1807, 1821, and 1832 detail Hogg's hard service as a child in the country, his struggles to become a literary man, and his later financial difficulties.

90(b) the metropolis Hogg visited London for nearly three months at the beginning of 1832.

90(b) O, my soul [...] united from Jacob's last words to Simeon and Levi in Genesis 49.6: 'O my soul, come not thou into their secret; unto their assembly, mine honour, be not thou united'.

Sermon IX. Marriage
text from I Corinthians 7.9.

91(b) "He that marrieth [...] doth *better.*" I Corinthians 7.38: 'So then he that giveth her in marriage doeth well; but he that giveth her not in marriage doeth better'.

91(b) "Marriage is honourable," Hebrews 13.4.

91(b) "Whosoever findeth a wife, findeth a good thing." see Proverbs 18.22.

91(b) The apostle the last quotation is from the book of Proverbs, supposedly written by the old testament king Solomon. The others are attributed to the apostle Paul in the Authorised Version of the Bible, although it is now believed that the Epistle to the Hebrews was not written by him.

91(c) the destruction of the old world an allusion to the unions between the sons of God and the daughters of men preceding Noah's flood in Genesis 6.1-7.

91(c) Isaac and Rebecca Genesis 26.34-35 relates that the marriages of Esau to Hittite women 'were a grief of mind unto Isaac and to Rebekah'.

91(c) brought the patriarch Judah into great trouble and iniquity Judah married a Canaanite woman, Shuah, and had three sons, two of whom were slain by God for wickedness. He also had twins by his daughter-in-law, Tamar, under the impression she was a prostitute—see Genesis 38.

91(c) a grievous curse on David David engineered the death of Uriah the Hittite and then married his widow Bathsheba, thus displeasing God—see II Samuel 11.

91(c) rent the kingdom of Israel from his grandson God declared to David's son Solomon that he would take the kingdom from his family and give it to his servant, as a punishment to him for going after other gods at the instigation of his foreign wives—see I Kings 11.1-13. Solomon's son Rehoboam lost the kingdom of Israel (the northern kingdom) to Jeroboam and kept only the kingdom of Judah (the southern kingdom, including Jerusalem)—see I Kings 12.1-20.

91(d) every man have his own wife, and every woman her own husband alluding to Paul's injunction in I Corinthians 7.2: 'Nevertheless, to avoid fornication, let every man have his own wife, and let every woman have her own husband'.

91(d) tried both ways a long time Hogg was forty-nine years old at the time of his marriage in 1820.

91(d) a far greater man this quotation has not been identified.

91(d) man and wife are one flesh an allusion to Matthew 19.6, 'they are no more twain, but one flesh'.

92(a) the primeval curse God's curse on Eve for persuading Adam to eat the forbidden fruit in Genesis 3.16: 'I will greatly multiply thy sorrow and thy conception; in sorrow thou shalt bring forth children; and thy desire shall be to thy husband, and he shall rule over thee'.

96(b) meetness fitness, suitability.

96(d) the gospel enjoins [...] bear one another's burdens see Galatians 6.2.

96(d) rejoice [...] them that weep see Romans 12.15.

96(d) to please every one his neighbour for his own good see Romans 15.2.

96(d) to be kind and tender-hearted, pitiful and courteous I Peter 3.8, 'love as brethren, be pitiful, be courteous'.

96(d) to support the weak, and to be patient towards all men Acts 20.35, 'so labouring ye ought to support the weak'.

96(d) fruits of this spirit Galatians 5.22-23: 'But the fruit of the Spirit is love, joy, peace, longsuffering, gentleness, goodness, faith, Meekness, temperance'.

97(b)–98(c) an extract from Irving [...] "Man is the creature [...] smitten it with decay." see Washington Irving, 'The Broken Heart', in *The Sketch Book of Geoffrey Crayon, Gent.*, new edition, 2 vols (London, 1821), I, 107-15 (pp.108-10). Hogg's long quotation is not exact.

97(c) the wings of the morning Psalm 139.9: 'If I take the wings of the morning, and dwell in the uttermost parts of the sea'.

Sermon X. Reviewers

text see Job 31.35: 'Oh, that one would hear me! behold my desire is, that the Almighty would answer me, and that mine adversary had written a book'.

99(b) Dean Swift the passage in which Swift refers to Job as a reviewer has not been identified.

99(b) Sir Walter Scott see the opening paragraph of Scott's review of Colonel T. Thornton's *A Sporting Tour through the Northern Parts of England, and great Part of the Highlands of Scotland* in the *Edinburgh Review*, 5 no.10 (January 1805), 398-400. Scott read this review to Hogg from manuscript, and Hogg says that the idea of Job as a reviewer 'was so ludicrous that I was like to die of laughing at it'—see *Anecdotes of Sir W. Scott*, ed. by Douglas S. Mack (Edinburgh: Scottish Academic Press, 1983), p.52.

99(b) Job says see Job 19.23.

99(b) by Moses the Pentateuch, or first five books of the Bible, are commonly attributed to Moses but not the book of Job.

99(b) his father-in-law after killing the Egyptian overseer Moses fled to Midian and married Zipporah, the daughter of Jethro, looking after his sheep for him— see Exodus 3.1.

99(c) the legitimate reviewer by the early 1830s the leading reviews such as the *Edinburgh Review* and *Quarterly Review* consisted of fewer and longer articles than previously, while weekly literary papers such as the *Literary Gazette* or *Athenaeum* increasingly dominated the business of getting out a wide range of reviews of recently-published books.

99(d) he who was long accounted the highest Hogg is perhaps referring here to Francis Jeffrey (1773-1850), the editor of the *Edinburgh Review* until 1829, and a leading spokesman for the Whigs.

100(c) thought, but never so well expressed Alexander Pope, 'An Essay on Criticism', lines 297-98: 'True wit is nature to advantage dressed,/ What oft was thought, but ne'er so well expressed'.

100(c) One generation [...] earth abideth ever see Ecclesiastes 1.4.

101(b) the compasses, the square, and the rule all instruments for precise measurement. Compare William Cowper, *Conversation* (1782): 'A poet does not work by square or line,/ As smiths and joiners perfect a design' (lines 789-90).

102(c) my uncle Toby from Laurence Sterne's *Tristram Shandy*, Book 6, Chapter 1. Sterne is commenting on those critics who attacked the earlier volumes of that work.

102(d)–103(a) since reviewing came in fashion Hogg is presumably referring back to the commencement of such periodicals as the *Monthly Review* (1749), *Critical Review* (1756), and *Edinburgh Review* (1802).

103(a) an adder in the path from Jacob's dying words to his sons in Genesis 49.17.

103(b) Moses [...] Job, David, and Isaiah referring to the early books in the old testament: i.e. the first five books of the Bible (attributed to Moses); the book of Job; the Psalms (attributed to David); and the book of Isaiah.

103(b) Homer the Greek epic poet regarded in antiquity as the author of *The Iliad* and *The Odyssey*, who probably lived in the ninth century BC.

103(b) Hesiod a Greek poet, probably of the eighth century BC and the author of 'Works and Days', which gives ethical maxims and practical instructions derived from his own rustic life.

103(b) Pindar a Greek lyric poet, born in either 522 or 518 BC and who is supposed to have lived to be eighty years old.

103(b) Ossian a Gaelic bard and warrior hero in Gaelic tradition, the son of Fingal. James Macpherson (1736-96) elaborated and re-created traditional Ossianic material in 'translations' that were immensely influential for early European Romanticism.

103(c) my own school Hogg once described himself to Scott as 'the king o' the mountain an' fairy school' (see *Familiar Anecdotes*, p.118), emphasising his own ground as supernatural legends and ballads of the kind that still survived, during his childhood, in Ettrick oral tradition.

103(d) the Modern Athens Edinburgh.

103(d) a certain little great man Francis Jeffrey (1773-1850), the editor of the *Edinburgh Review* until 1829, was barely five feet tall. Hogg makes a similar allusion to him in 'Will and Sandy. A Scots Pastoral', in *A Queer Book*, ed. by P. D. Garside (Edinburgh: Edinburgh University Press, 1995), p.178.

104(a) pinning your faith to another man's sleeve taking his assertion for granted– in medieval times a man's followers wore his badge on their sleeves, but as it was easily removed or changed it could be a deceptive sign.

104(a) a great evil under the sun see Ecclesiastes 5.13 and note to 89(b).

106(b) Save by translations Hogg often quotes Latin in his written works, which suggests the possibility that (despite his assertion here) he eventually acquired some rudimentary knowledge of the language–see, for example, *Memoir*, p.135.

106(d) the lays of Ossian [...] in their original tongue Hogg clearly had some knowledge of Gaelic, however slight, for he reproduces phrases of Gaelic phonetically in a number of his works–see, for example, 'Julia M,Kenzie' in *Tales of the Wars of Montrose*, ed. by Gillian Hughes (Edinburgh: Edinburgh University Press, 1996), pp.138-53 and notes.

Sermon XI. Deistical Reformers
text Psalm 14.1.

108(b) deist a person who accepts the existence of God on the evidence of reason but rejects revealed religion.

108(c) as the sparks fly upward Job 5.7: 'Yet man is born unto trouble, as the sparks fly upward'.

108(c) a local habitation and a name Shakespeare, *A Midsummer Night's Dream*, V.1.16-17, 'and gives to airy nothing/ A local habitation and a name'.

109(a) Rowism John McLeod Campbell (1800-1876), minister of the parish of Rowe, or Rhu, near Helensburgh in Scotland, was deposed for heresy in 1831. He was uncomfortable with the calvinist doctrine of election, and preached 'Universal Atonement through Christ, pardon for sins freely offered to all men as the ground of Assurance without which there is no saving faith'–see J. H. S. Burleigh, *A Church History of Scotland* (London: Oxford University Press, 1960, repr. 1973), p.332.

110(a) our God and our guide [...] rich rewarder this amalgamation of Psalm 48.14 and Genesis 15.1 is evidently characteristic of the allusive prayers offered in domestic worship. The prayer imitated by Duncan in 'History of Duncan Campbell', *The Spy*, No. 51 (17 August 1811), pp.401-08 (p.402) is very similarly worded.

110(b) "I would rather [...] moon," see Shakespeare's *Julius Caesar*, IV.2.79.

110(b) our Saviour, and [...] that Comforter two of the persons of the Trinity: Jesus Christ is the Saviour, and, according to John 14.26, the Holy Ghost is the Comforter.

110(c) O fools [...] slow of heart from Christ's words to the disciples at Emmaus– see Luke 24.25.

113(c) Ode to the Devil the quotation which follows is an extract from Hogg's own 'Hymn to the Devil' sung by Prig, Prim, and Pricker, in *The Three Perils of Man*, ed. by Douglas Gifford (Edinburgh and London: Scottish Academic Press, 1972), pp.294-96.

114(a) a flim and a flam a *flim* is apparently Hogg's own coining, probably from 'flim-flam', a piece of nonsense or idle talk. A *flam* is a sham or deception, a caprice or whim.

116(b) the simple rule of Scripture Matthew 7.14: 'Ye shall know them by their fruits'.

116(d)–117(a) Where wast thou [...] waves be stayed? see Job 38.4-11.

117(a-b) Hell is naked [...] who can understand? see Job 26.6-14.

117(b-c) He bowed the heavens [...] breath of thy nostrils see Psalm 18.9-15.

117(c) When I consider [...] all the earth! see Psalm 8.3-4, 9.

117(c-d) The heavens declare [...] to run his race see Psalm 19.1-5.

117(d) those men the prophecies concerning the Messiah were made by writers of the old testament who, obviously, lived before the time of Christ.

118(c) in the wilderness Hogg's home was at Altrive Lake in Yarrow, still a remote rural district.

118(c) annealed tempered by exposure to fire.

118(d) gall of bitterness and bond of iniquity from Peter's rebuke to Simon for offering money for the powers of the Holy Ghost, in Acts 8.23.

119(a) rather take our chance [...] nothing this famous argument is known as Pascal's Wager: the French mathematician and moralist Blaise Pascal (1623–62) argued that it is rational to believe in God, for if one believes in God and the belief is false then one has lost nothing, whereas if one believes in God and it is true a great good is gained.

119(b) sunny braes [...] barren wastes a pastoral allusion, not totally dissimilar to various shepherds' prayers in Hogg's own fiction: see, for example, Daniel Bell's extended comparison of his daughter Gatty to a ewe-lamb in *The Three Perils of Woman*, ed. David Groves, Antony Hasler, and Douglas S. Mack (Edinburgh: Edinburgh University Press, 1995), p.184.

119(b) neither a shadow from the heat, nor a shelter from the storm an allusion to Isaiah 25.4.

119(c) like the beasts that perish a phrase from Psalm 49.12.

119(c) Almighty Physician Jesus alludes to himself as a physician in incidents recorded in Matthew 9.12 and Luke 4.23.

119(d) sun, the moon, and stars [...] changed a partial paraphrase of Psalm 102.25–26.